ANCHOR
OF MY HEART

Memories of a Cape Breton Childhood

Derrick Nearing, MMM, CD

 FriesenPress

Suite 300 - 990 Fort St
Victoria, BC, V8V 3K2
Canada

www.friesenpress.com

ISBN
978-1-5255-1197-4 (Hardcover)
978-1-5255-1198-1 (Paperback)
978-1-5255-1199-8 (eBook)

1. BIOGRAPHY & AUTOBIOGRAPHY, PERSONAL MEMOIRS

Distributed to the trade by The Ingram Book Company

DEDICATION

This collection is dedicated to my late mother and father, Patricia and Fred Nearing, who lovingly nudged and guided me throughout my childhood into adulthood. To my siblings, Kim, Kevin, Andrea, and our late sister Carolee, who were all there as an important part of these stories throughout my childhood. Finally, this book is dedicated to those family and friends who came into my life as a child in Cape Breton.

ANCHOR HEART

Memories of a Cape Breton Childhood

CONTENTS

FOREWORD

THE IDEA OF WRITING A COLLECTION OF STORIES OF MY CHILD-hood began two years ago with a simple opportunity to submit a bi-weekly story for the New Waterford Community Press. In doing this, I serendipitously tapped into a longing for my past, which many readers also understood and wanted me to share. With the opportunity for a weekly submission, this gave me a unique chance to look more closely into the culture I grew up in, and around my old neighbourhood, and the town of New Waterford on beautiful Cape Breton Island. To look at how these seemingly simple, everyday encounters had come to shade all aspects of my life.

When I left my home in Cape Breton all those years ago, the decision to leave was not without much thought and deliberation. However, the decision was made for me by the economics on Cape Breton Island at the time. With few job opportunities available and a declining population, it was sadly time for me to leave and seek a life elsewhere, one of the hardest decisions I have ever made.

The writing of these stories pays tribute to those who have helped form my worldview along the way, which has anchored me in everything I've been through up to this day. The metaphor of an anchor seemed an appropriate when I began writing about my childhood, for this is what our childhood memories are to us as we grow older, anchoring us with a moral compass, safely navigating us throughout our lives.

I was privileged to grow up when and where I did, within the rich culture of Cape Breton art, music and its heritage, the hardworking values I witnessed displayed daily by the men and women who were in my life, and the simplicity of being a child during this time. It was times such as visiting my Nanny in Dominion on Sunday's, eating her homemade bread as she took it out of the oven, or encounters with people of integrity such as the teachers at St Agnes School, playing on the high school soccer team or most anywhere I went during these times. I witnessed the character of my parents who, through hard work and sacrifice, raised my brothers and sisters and gave us the best life they could, never complaining about their lot in life, just wanting us to do better. I observed in the adults around my neighbourhood and throughout Cape Breton, an unwavering loyalty and dedication to family, which has served as the foundation for my personal values and work ethic, which I have embraced and followed throughout my life.

I've been fortunate to have been taught a sense of modesty, family, and loyalty, with a large dose of common sense. These lessons, and the examples given to me throughout my childhood, were later internalized and adapted, greatly influencing me to become who I am today. As I transition to my later years, these memories continue to influence and give meaning to me as I move though life.

In the Welsh language, there is a word which encapsulates how I have felt since leaving my home, this word is "Hiraeth". Hiraeth roughly translates into a homesickness for a place or time that was, a time you can never return to, a longing and a sense of loss for those places and times of your past. Some thirty-five years have passed since I left Cape Breton to join the Canadian Forces, during this time not a day has passed where I don't have a longing for those times and people who weaved in and out of my life. My Cape Breton childhood has given me a unique perspective all these years later, with the passage of time and reflecting on those times, I now see what matters in life. Perhaps it is only later in our lives when we can look back at our childhood and come to fully appreciate the simpler things such as family, friends, the good times as well as bad. In the end, it is in these simple human interactions where we define ourselves and for all those things which made me who I am, this is my longing, my "Hiraeth."

ACKNOWLEDGEMENTS

I COULDN'T HAVE DONE THIS WITHOUT THOSE FRIENDS AND MENTORS who have provided guidance and love through this process: Dr. Paul Munson, who started me on this journey by introducing me to the idea of writing to keep my memories alive. Dr. John Whelan, who has encouraged and guided me over the last couple of years with reviewing some of my stories and suggesting ways to improve. Marillyn Saffery, who has given me guidance as to ways to evoke the emotional side in the telling of these stories. My friend Stephan Tremblay, who has been a source of calmness and encouragement for me throughout this process. My friend and mentor, Steve Merriman, who patiently listened to me as I spoke about how I wanted to approach the writing this collection of short stories, making positive suggestions for the way forward, always constructive and encouraging, many thanks to you. There are many others I may have missed, for this I apologize in advance, but also thank you for your help with my stories. It is these people who patiently listened to stories about my love for Cape Breton, nudging me into writing them down to share with others. Those friends who were continually there offering help and guidance, and in a way, they were *my* anchor reminding me of these times I wrote of. I want to give a special thanks to Darren O'Quinn, editor of The New Waterford Community Press, for having faith in me and publishing my short stories the last couple of years.

Thanks to those in my hometown of New Waterford, who through kind words of support over the last couple of years, have encouraged me to take this step and move forward with the publication of these stories. Please enjoy them as they grease the wheels to your own memories, since in the end these stories are not mine, but *ours*.

Finally, this collection would have not occurred without the love, support, and encouragement from my wife, Maureen, and my children, Hannah and Reilly, without whose patience and encouragement I could have never completed this offering of short stories.

COPS AND ROBBERS

ITS FUNNY NOW WHEN I LOOK BACK AT MY CHILDHOOD, HOW WE were all brought up to be comfortable with penknives, pellet guns and toys of this sort. Having my own kids now and volunteering at their school, I have noticed that the kids of today have little or no familiarity with pen knives or BB guns and roughhousing certainly no longer tolerated. This type of play now frowned upon, but not back in the days of my youth. It was the norm during my childhood experiences.

I still remember the retired coal miners who would sit on the little concrete step in front of the St Agnes Parish Hall Annex as they spoke for hours. The one thing they did the entire time was to whittle away the hours, while they were speaking. There were usually the same three or four retired coal miners, Capwire, Stem, Mickey and Dan Willie. They would sit there for hours upon hours and talk about the coal mine's or what was commonly known as "pit talk". I noticed all the time while standing there, they each had their pen knives out whittling wood. By the time they would finish their chat, a couple of hours later, there would be wood chips everywhere. But never was the pen or pocket knife associated with violence or danger in my experiences growing up. To me it was always a handy thing to have when a piece of tape or rope had to be cut and you had this in your pocket. There were times when someone would need a bottle opened and you would have the opener on your knife for this. It was just a handy little tool to have and no one seemed to mind back then. In retrospect, I believe it was the fact that we all had a little pocket or pen knife and they were familiar to us, we all knew to respect them and not abuse them, as we knew our parents would take them away from us.

I'm not sure if we didn't know any better or if it was the fact that many of our parents were very practical and had themselves come through WWII and after this period, a penknife or toy gun didn't seem so threatening. I remember in the back yard with my friends, Bobby and Chris, playing with toy guns and pretending to be "Joe Mannix" or "Frank Cannon". We would run around with our Cap guns and pretend we were shooting one another, with one of us taking our turn in the role of Mannix, while the others would take on the role of the bad guys, of course Mannix or Cannon would always get their man and win in the end.

Looking at the way we were raised, there was no fear or worry from our parents about us growing up being violent or overly aggressive. There was seemingly an abundance of toy guns which we played with, as well as penknives.

I still remember one birthday when I was 4 or 5 years old, mom and dad got me a set of toy guns with a holster for each hip, just as I imagined the cowboys had back in the frontier days. They had gotten me two silver pistols, made of heavy metal, and had a spring-loaded compartment on top, when you pushed the button it would pop open. It would be in this compartment where you would load in a roll of gun powder caps and pull the first few to the back of the gun so it would be fed upwards as you pulled the trigger. The caps were little rolls of red paper with every quarter inch a little black dot of gunpowder and when you pulled the trigger the hammer would hit the powder then a small flash would occur, a puff of smoke and smell of gunpowder as it fired. We loved it as we played and rolled around in the high grass in the fields down by the brook, letting our imaginations take us back to those days of the wild west.

I think it was when I was about 8 years old and on the last day of school in grade 3, I got a potato gun! Now, the great thing about this type of toy gun was all you needed was a potato for your ammunition. What you had to do was push the end of the gun into the potato, twist then aim and shoot. It was only the build up of air pressure inside the gun that caused the little piece of potato to pop out as you pulled the trigger. It came out with only minimal force behind it, so no damage to anyone was ever done.

I also remember those little hard plastic guns, you would squeeze the trigger continuously until inside the clear green plastic you would see a metal wheel spinning around, rubbing against a flint causing sparks to fly out the end of the barrel. There was a distinctive smell of metal along with this. When we used these toys, we would imagine ourselves to be space travellers, unlike the cap guns, they were a little more exotic and futuristic. We would play with these all day long and for it would never seem to get boring.

Those days growing up in New Waterford we were only doing things that little boys did. We were playing with toys at the time children could play with, and in fact were given by parents and relatives, while at the same time this playing was also serving to teach each of us to respect the potential danger that they also possessed. No one, I can remember, ever got hurt or injured and in the end, we were no worse for these experiences throughout our childhood.

HEELAN STREET TOT LOT

W E PRESENTLY LIVE ACROSS FROM A PLAYGROUND AND often when listening to the children play, it takes me back to my own days playing at our neighbourhood "Tot Lot" in New Waterford. Looking back, what amazes me from that time is how busy the playgrounds would get with the slow build up of children. It would begin with a small child's laugh breaking the silence on a quiet Saturday morning, the squeaking of a swing in a rhythmical pattern as the swing went back and forth. My mind drifts back to my hometown and of how the little chain linked fence tot lot on Heelan Street was the centre of my early childhood. How many memoires were made there over the years, how during the summer months we waited by the gates for the Summer student workers to show up and unlock them, so we could get in to play until it closed at days end.

Anyone from this era can remember that playgrounds back then were not the nice smooth, prefabricated, triple safety inspected ones we see in today's playgrounds. There was no sand, rubber mats or soft wood chips for us to land in as there is today. Most times at the bottom of the slides and around the play structures, it was good old gravel or perhaps a little sand, which would dig into our knees and scratch our knees, legs, and backs as we slid, jumped and fell, but never a complaint was heard as we were too immersed in having fun to realize it should hurt.

As a kid in the late 1960's I remember the tot lot at the bottom of our street, there were similar tot lots all over new Waterford, every neighbourhood had one, surrounded by fences which opened in the morning, then locked at the end of each day. Funny thing looking back, is how every summer how we couldn't wait for it to be opened every day early in the morning beginning on the last day of school and lasting until the first day of the new school year.

I remember one Summer, I must have been only 8 or 9 and the teenage students hired to run the tot lot that Summer were Brenda and Mary Helen, each morning they would show up with a couple of buckets of sports equipment and other activities for the kids. We would all be waiting at the gates and as soon as the gates opened we would run in and the day begun, I recall that there was a morning session and an afternoon one with us going home for a half hour at lunch. At days end the tot lot would be locked up until the next day.

First thing I would do would be run to the "Spinner Wheel" otherwise known as a roundabout (or merry-go-round). This was one of those playground apparatuses which today has been banned because of the inherent dangers with it, but it was good enough for the kids of our generation. We would all grab a spot by a bar on the spinner, then a couple of us would run until it was spinning like a bat out of hell, then try to hop onto it as It spun. Of course, we would all get dizzy, then someone would fall off and get a good wack to the back of the head or a face plant, while another kid would try to stop the spinner and fall off as their knees dragged on the hard ground tearing their new jeans, which would always impress the parents.

After this I would head over to the high slide, made of metal, and burning hot in the summers sun, its rough and rusty metal edges were Tetanus shot worthy. To my 8-year-old self, the top of the slide looked as though it was 50 feet in the air as I ascended to the top, the ladder which had no safety basket around it or grips was my only way up, the rungs shiny and slippery from all the times kids' shoes had rubbed on them. Climbing up the ladder it seemed to go higher and higher with no protection around me, I felt as if I could fall at any time. I got to the top and with the sun in my eyes and wind in my face, sat down on the top platform and from here I could see Brenda and Mary Helen playing games with the kids, others on the spinner, see-saw and monkey bars. I felt as though I was on top of the world, then reaching forward and grabbing the two bars on either side of the slide, I would propel myself downward. I was thrilled with the quick slide to the bottom, suddenly there was a bump at the end, knees hitting the sand. It was then I discovered that this was actually fun, forget about the knees or that it hurt hitting the ground, I wanted to have those butterflies again from the rush of going down the slide. Off to the top again I headed, waiting my turn.

Then it was from the slide onto the 'See Saw" or "teeter-totter" I always liked the see saw, but it seemed most times I couldn't get someone of equal size to get on with me, either it would be a kid too small and I would have to go slow so I did catapult him off on the way up or crack his teeth when hitting the ground. I found out one day why they called it the teeter totter, I was on with a bigger guy and we were going up and down when suddenly a friend of his came over and they held me up in the air, suspended for a moment, then suddenly both let go and I quickly hit the ground with my face smashing in to the handgrips and a tooth was knocked out. I ran home to the comfort of my mom, with tooth in hand, but fortunately it was only a milk tooth.

Then there was the swing set, for sure this could be a tooth losing experience for both the rider as well as unsuspecting kids walking by while daydreaming in front of the swings. I recall sitting and beginning with the pumping of my feet and legs, leaning back on the way forward and forward on the way back. I'm sure we never realized the physics involved in making it go faster, higher, or how to slow it down, but it was always fun to just sit there and pump your feet and the higher you swung, the more butterflies that would be in your stomach. Once I got the hang of it by watching the other older kids and learned how to jump from the swing as it was moving forward running as I jumped off. First, I had to pay the price for this knowledge with a few face plantings or getting the swing off the back of the head because of a jump too soon or too late, as I didn't quite understand the concept of how to jump off the swing. However, being a quick study, I got the knack of it and could jump off with the best of them and as soon as my feet touched the ground my forward momentum would have me running away from the swing as it was coming back.

Then there were the monkey bars which were open at each end and had a metal horizontal ladder as you tried to make your way across you hung over a sand gravel mix beneath you. As with all the other playground apparatus, they were made from industrial metal and in the hot summer sun would blister your hands, arms, and legs as you crawled and climbed on them. I think the fun was in hanging upside down and letting the blood pool in your head, but the other thing was when the tot lot supervisors weren't looking you would wrap your legs around another kid's midsection and try to pull them off, even as your arms stretched and pain settled in. It was a battle to see who would let go first, all in good fun. There were also the metal gymnastic rings which hung on long chains from overhead bars, this was another old-time playground apparatus now considered a safety hazard. Perhaps this is partly because kids used to do things such as hang from the rings and swing and bash into one another, or hang upside down from their feet and occasionally getting their foot caught in the ring and then would need a couple older kids to push them up so they could free their feet.

Of course, there were other things on the go during the day with skipping ropes, a game of baseball or catch, but mostly we would just play until the end of the day and all go home tired and extremely happy with the days fun.

Although now an adult, far from the freedom and innocence of childhood, I think it important to reflect upon these times of our youth and remember the wind in our face and sun in our eyes as we played, carefree and happy, oblivious to the adult world. We should all try going back to these times, if only for a moment in our mind, go to that tot lot on Heelan Street or those at Central, Scotchtown and Mount Carmel Schools, let your memories take you back to this magical time of youth and innocence. Remember what made you happy then and if life seems to have gotten heavy, then go back and remember it doesn't always have to be heavy.

As a child, I never understood the benefit of failing, benefit of having to try repeatedly for days on end, until I got it just right as with the swing, but then again maybe this is the way its suppose to be. To fail, fall flat on your face, then have the self determination to pick yourself up and be a smarter and stronger child, who later becomes a stronger and smarter adult. Every day on the playground was different from the one before, never two days the same as you lived the story of your childhood, but for me that was ok, I couldn't control these things and this is the great thing about being a child, every day is a new experience, a new lesson. For just today, even only for the time it takes to read this story, go back to that innocent time as a child when the only worry was play, making mistakes, learning and friends, these are the times of our lives.

A HOME IS FAMILY

TRAVELLING BACK HOME TO CAPE BRETON IN THE SUMMER OF 2011, I knew it would be difficult. I was driving back to help my mother deal with the heartbreaking news of having a terminal cancer. I was returning to help her with the preparation of a will, settling her business and other end of life issues which she wanted cared for. Her illness was sudden, unexpected and discovered only a couple of weeks earlier, time was of the essence as it was a rapidly progressing cancer. The whole event began to unfold a couple of weeks earlier, she had been taken out to enjoy a meal at a local restaurant with my sister Carolee, and her fiancé John. While eating, she went into convulsions and had what looked like a grand mal seizure and was rushed to hospital. After a CT scan, it would be found out that it was in fact brain cancer, which had now spread throughout her body. She was informed that it was very aggressive and to prepare her personal business and say her good byes, when I was told of this I understood her time would be short with us. I requested the time off from work to be there for her and drove home immediately from my military base in Petawawa, Ontario.

While driving back to Cape Breton, a twenty-three-hour drive from my home in Pembroke, I had an abundance of time alone to think about what was going on with mom and it began to settle in. With time being compressed, I wanted to spend as much of the remaining time with her, feel her love in my birth home, and to be there to help her transition from this life to her final resting place. I had all these thoughts racing around in my mind and little time to catch my breath. When I finally arrived, walking in the front door, there she was sitting in her chair, her big old sofa chair she had sat in most of the time l was growing up. Looking at her and how she wanted so badly to get discharged from the hospital to come home, it was then when I began to understand why she loved the old home on Heelan Street, why this place meant so much to her.

Spending those final two weeks with mom before her passing, I knew this would be my last chance to make one more memory with her, one more memory to add to the tapestry that was my childhood in this old house. It would be bittersweet, saying goodbye to her in those last days as I attended to her final wishes. Mom asked me to have Fr. Doucette come to the house to talk with her and help prepare for her death. I called and spoke to him and told him what was taking place, with my mother, and that she wanted to speak with him and get things in order before her passing. It was difficult for me, as this was one of the final steps one does in the preparation of your death, with this came the realization that she was accepting her fate and wanted to prepare for it. When Fr. Doucette arrived, I went to his car and greeted him as mom waited inside to meet with him, as he went in to speak with her I sat on the front veranda so that no one would interrupt, so they would have enough time to talk. I was alone to my thoughts sitting on the front step, when suddenly I was overcome with emotion, realizing what was going on and the finality of this moment. These sad but necessary moments were now part of the kaleidoscope of memories that once were my mom, dad, brothers, sisters, and neighbours in our small but comfortable house we called home.

As I spent the last week with mom, those memories from child-hood came flooding back. I felt the pressure of time ticking away and I needed a little more, just to sit and talk to mom a little longer and add onto those last few memories, time became ever more pressing, as death was close by waiting. When she finally passed I had no time to mourn, I found myself quickly into the planning and preparing for her funeral, the Mass and burial. With all my brothers and sister now returning home for mom's funeral, once again the house became a center of activity, a sort of rallying point for family, cousins, friends, and neighbours wishing to say their final farewells to her. I watched everyone during this time and came to slowly realize that this would be our last time all together as brothers and sisters in the home we had been brought up in.

Once everything was completed and mom laid to rest, everyone went back to their homes and I was now alone to myself in the old homestead. As I went upstairs looking around my old bedroom one last time the room was empty. This old house had been a rock for our family and the rooms which that made up the house were never judgmental, they didn't preach to us when we made mistakes, and could keep the best of secrets when they witnessed a first kiss or a parents' argument. It is all of this and so much more that makes our old home on Heelan Street what it was. It wasn't a big house, only nine hundred square feet with the seven of us living there. It wasn't fancy, but in my mind's eye, it was elegant enough. It was the most beautiful of places to be on those lazy summer days, with the light coming in the front picture window as it was filtered through the leaves on the white birch tree in the front yard facing Heelan Street.

As I looked out the front window, I came to realize that as we grow older we can never go back. Once we grow up and leave home we begin to create our own lives and are left with the memories of what was from those times. My growing up in Cape Breton had made me realize that within all the homes of my friends, neighbours, and family all over Cape Breton Island, that they had been built on love and respect. Homes weren't as much planned as they were decorated and dressed up by significant family and life events as they were taking place.

Over the years, as we go from babies to children, teenagers to adults, our homes are gradually built from the first lock of hair from that first haircut, our first Christmas carol book we brought home our first year in primary school. Slowly but surely, these events, the good and bad, are all weaved into our homes and into our lives, making a beautiful tapestry. Little by little, story by story, and upset by upset, the foundation was slowly laid over our time as children. Later, when we cried, laughed, shared stories within the four walls that made up our home, the story of the family was flushed out and the home was at the centre of it all.

Finally, I understood why my mother always wanted to be home, she never liked to travel outside Cape Breton or be away from home for very long. This old home on Heelan Street was her safe space, it was a place where there was no badness for her, she controlled her world within these four walls. Caring for mom during her last days, gave me time to reflect on those times we were all together as a family, memories of the good times and hard times, gently softened with the passage of time. It was with this knowledge that as children, being raised in this house, mom would always be there for us when one of us came home crying with a scraped knee, hurt feelings, it was the security knowing she would always be there for us.

In those last few minutes before driving back to Pembroke, I knew that this would likely be my last trip home. As I stood there, looking around at the house, now empty of everything I had known for years, my mind was unable to focus with so many memories flooding back. I was trying to take in those last few minutes before leaving. I was at a point where I wanted to get into my car and drive away, but something was holding me there. I went back into the house and up the stairs, looked at my old bedroom one more time, I sat on my old bed and my eyes scanned the room as I was thinking of all the years of being raised here. Looking around there were posters from my high school years still on the walls, the old record player over in the corner by my desk where I would study those long nights preparing for exams. I then stood up and walked to the window, which from my bedroom I use to look out and see the old coal mine, Number 12 Colliery, I imagined watching my dad walking down West Avenue to the coal mine. As I left the bedroom, closing the door behind me, I went downstairs and walked once more into the kitchen where mom made all those great meals for all those occasions, then into the family room, finally the living room. There was nothing left for me to see, it was now so quiet and lifeless without mom there. I was prolonging this moment, the moment I never wanted to arrive, the moment I had to leave. As I walked out the front door closing it behind me for the last time and hearing the door lock "click", I didn't want to look back.

I got into my car to begin the long drive back to my home in Pembroke, Ontario. Driving up Heelan Street, my throat began to tighten up, I had difficulty swallowing and my eyes began to well up with tears. Then, with a terrible emptiness in the pit of my stomach, I realized that my heart was broken and finally coming to understand,

and accept the finality of this loss, the loss of everything that was, I was leaving home for the last time.

As the house became smaller and smaller in my rear-view mirror, I realized that I had to move forward. I still had my own family in Pembroke to care for. One may never fully get over the loss of one's mother or father, but we need to move forward, to live our own lives as they had lived theirs. Looking through the rear-view window one more time, the house was now only a tiny spot on the horizon, with the ocean as its a backdrop. I knew it was time to cherish the memories I had made but move forward and live my life, love my family.

As for that old comfortable home on Heelan Street, it too will eventually get over the loss of its family, and hopefully someday a young couple will move in, have children, and raise them, making all those memories all over again in the comfort of a well-worn home.

RAISED TO
BE PRACTICAL

WHEN I WAS A KID AND THERE WAS WORK AROUND THE house to be done, such as carpentry or plumbing or something essential needed to be fixed, our fathers would usually be the ones to do these tasks. If there was a window to be replaced, again, mom or dad would be there for this as well. This was the case with everything from household needs to fixing the car. When I explain this way of living to my children, they say to me, "Dad, that sounds so old fashioned and boring." I understand from a kid's point of view why they say this, and why they may see it as too "boring", but why? Well, for us as kids it wasn't boring because there were no electronics or computers of any type growing up back then. The truth is I wouldn't trade the way it was for anything and I don't think most of us from this time would. Looking back, I think we were all given a very sound and practical upbringing, which has served all of us well through all phases of our lives.

Growing up on Heelan Street at our home, dad worked full time at the coal mine and mom was a stay at home mother. This scene was repeated in nearly every home throughout Cape Breton. As kids, we often went out to play in the morning, not returning until last light, making up our own play and fun. One thing every kid did at one time or another growing up was to build a cabin in the backyard, or in the woods behind the coal mine. We had learned from our fathers how to use a hand saw or bow saw early in our childhood, how to use a claw hammer and how to draw out nails from the old wood, straighten them out on a brick for reuse. I think all the kid's, I grew up and played with, had these basic skills back then.

When I tell my younger friends how we were raised in Cape Breton as a child during the 1960's, with a "kids should be seen and not heard" philosophy, many don't like or understand this statement. But it served an important purpose in our upbringing. What it did, mostly, was teach us to quiet ourselves and be patient, listen to our parents and adults, to learn to watch and observe what was happening before asking questions. For the most part, with dad working in the coal mine and mom busy around the house, we were usually left as kids to our own devices. With the expectation to entertain ourselves, we would be developing our imaginations, exploring, and continually trying and experimenting with things, failing then figuring out why we failed and finally with enough attempts success would ultimately come. It was a time of innocence and free play, and I believe, will never be seen again by any future generations who come after us.

I still remember so many of us who had built cabins back in those days. They wouldn't have passed the building inspector's rigors at the time, but boy were they were fun to build, and to sneak off to when you're a little kid. I had my own cabin in the back corner of our yard. My father had a wood pile in our back yard, so one day I got to building a cabin with Bobby. We gathered all the two-by-fours from the pile of wood and then went looking for nails. We couldn't find any, so began to draw the nails out of the wood, and got a couple old bricks and started to straighten them out and put them in an old Export A tobacco can. Once we had the nails, we began to build. It was built to fit! No measuring for the most part, just approximations by holding one piece up to the last one to see if it was "close enough." Once it was all framed up, we would have to go on the hunt to scrounge up some old plywood to finish it. Sometimes we would go to Irish brook and there would be some there by the water, we would fish it out and carry it back home and add it. Other times, we would sneak into the coal yard to see what was there.

We would work on this for a day or two, and when finished, would have a great sense of pride in our efforts. Imagine, from start to finish, no adults around to supervise. A couple of kids who planned, gathered materials, and execute the building of a little cabin. Looking back, it was only a small little building, but for us it was a huge accomplishment. I can't remember if I ever had any pictures taken of the soap box cars, cabins, or hockey nets we built to play street hockey with on 2nd Street, but I sure can remember building so many things with my friends back then. Whenever we needed something for a game or event, we just got to it and built what was needed, never asking our parents for store bought items as it seemed more fun to just build what we needed at the time.

I wonder how many of todays parents would allow their children to go off alone, as we were, to go off by ourselves, walking to the pump house out at the Waterford Lake a couple of miles away? Along with a gang of boys early in the morning, only to return late in the afternoon. Swimming and playing all day, left to our own devices to entertain ourselves, and making the trip out and back along the train tracks from No. 12 Mine. I remember one time, one of the guys found a large sac of frog eggs out at the pump house. He had discovered it attached to some bullrushes and reeds, by the intake pipe at the pump house near the tracks. There it was, a big bag of jelly with hundreds of little black specks (frog embryos) all throughout the gelatinous mass. Some of the older boys said to leave it there, but of course one of the guys to put it into an old pickle jar and take it home so he could watch what would take place. It was brought it in the following Monday to school and over the weeks to follow, we would watch the black specks grow, until one morning we came to school, and finally the eggs were hatched into little pollywogs. Later into frogs and we would watch over time as their tails would slowly disappear.

Yes, I think it true that we will never see these days again. Some may think this a good thing, while others not. With todays computers and modern technological advances, kids don't have to make cabins, hockey nets or go carts. Today, everything from cabins to costumes all arrives for the kids pre-fabricated and pre-made, with little need to fire up the imagination or put much effort into improvising and working through some difficulty, without the aid of parents around to guide them. I think with many advances unfortunately comes some practical losses. I can only say that I am glad to have had a childhood where independence, imagination, and self reliance was the order of the day.

GRADING DAY

REMEMBER THE LAST FEW WEEKS OF THE SCHOOL YEAR WHEN I WENT to St. Agnes Elementary back in 1970, I was in grade 3. It was the usual routine a week or so before the end of the school year, make a class trip to either Fortress Louisburg, the Alexander Graham Bell museum, or Miners Museum in Glace Bay. All of us would be asked to bring in fifty cents each to pay for the bus, which doesn't seem like a lot today, but even back then some even had difficulty getting this much for a trip.

When the day came we would have a lunch packed from home, show up at school a half hour early, and then be loaded onto the old yellow school bus and we were off. This trip would signal the final week of school, and building of excitement with all of us knowing that soon it would all be over for the Summer. Our time being sequestered over the last ten months, within the walls of St. Agnes School, was nearing its end. Soon, we would be released to neighbourhoods all over town to explore and enjoy the two months of Summer off.

I remember that last day of my grade three that year vividly. It would be a time for growth, but it would take me many years into my adult life to appreciate the important lessons this day was about to give. It was an early start on that last day of school, and I tossed and turned as I tried to sleep the night before. The biggest thing on everyone's mind was their report card. If you passed every subject, but failed in one course, say math or English, then there was summer school. It was usually it was in Glace Bay, and it was your opportunity to make up that course so you could progress to the next grade level.

In those times schools and parents would decide whether to have a child repeat a grade if necessary, we always had one or two repeat a grade when I went to school, but never worried about this myself. Most kids knew by this time whether they were going to pass or not, but I was never too keen on school, and right up until I graduated from high school at BEC, I would put in just enough work to make the grade. I'm not sure why this was, it wasn't that I couldn't do the work, but I found it was boring, and couldn't focus. More importantly, it would only be later in life when I would realize how important education was and finally settle down and thrive in my studies. But first, I had to pay penance for my inability to focus and work.

On the last day, we were all called into class after morning recess. We knew that school was over at noon, and the enthusiasm to be free for the Summer was palpable in the air. We were like wild horses, ready to break out. Mrs. Aucoin called our names alphabetically, and as each of us was called, we would walk to the front of the class and get the envelope with our report card in it. As Mrs. Aucoin began passing out all the grading day cards, and I watched her face as she did this, one by one, alphabetically, slowly, each of us would be called to her desk and receive the brown envelope.

As they approached her desk, she would smile at each of the students and say, "Have a good summer and see you in September!" With my last name beginning with "N," I was one of the last to be called, and by the time she got to me, there was no longer a smile on her face. Suddenly Ms. Aucoin's face became more serious, and I could feel butterflies in my stomach it was then I realized something was up. As I approached, I started praying in my head the "Our Father," then quickly into a "Hail Mary", then I asked God to help me, to come down and somehow magically get into the envelope and save me from certain failure. But it was not to be, and I was to repeat grade three the following year. I remember that I cried a little on the way home, half with disappointment, and half with embarrassment for what mom and dad would think of my shortcomings.

I walked home after school, and the usual fifteen-minute walk took some hour or so to complete. I meandered all the way home going to the brook, then back towards the coal mine and walking down Ellsworth Avenue, it was an aimless walk and I was trying to figure out why this had happened to me, "I have to repeat grade three, why?" I thought to myself. I was crushed with the shock of having to repeat grade three again, and a little embarrassed when thinking of all my friends moving forward on to grade four and me left behind with kids' younger than myself. I didn't deserve this, I did well enough on all my work in school I thought and couldn't figure out why I was being kept back. When I walked in, mom and dad asked me how I did, and I ran over to mom and put my head on her shoulders and began sobbing, through the crying, I told her I had failed grade three and had to repeat it again. Mom hugged me and wiped away the tears and told me, "Its okay, Derrick. It will be all right." Comforting words from a mother.

Dad said to me, "Derrick, this is what happens when you didn't work hard and focus on the important things. So next year, remember this day." These were words I never forgot, but it would take many years to fully understand them. Mom told me that she and dad had spoken to the school, who were going to let me go to the next grade as my grades were good enough, but the recommendation from the teacher and principal was that it might be best for me to repeat the grade. Apparently, I was too immature and didn't play with the others well enough. My parents went with the recommendation to be kept back, I was confused, I did well enough to pass but my independence was a negative and I should be punished for this by being kept back, in my 8-year-old brain this made no sense.

Looking back, I must say that this little setback, although terrible to me at the time, didn't negatively affect me in the long term. It didn't damage me with the rest of my peers moving forward. Possibly I really did just need a little more time to mature, perhaps I needed this as a wake-up call to help gain a better understanding of how to focus in class. Whatever the reason, it gave me a little more time to learn the fundamentals of what I may have missed the year previous, and gave me time to mature a little more.

As children, we don't always have a full appreciation of these events, and it is often only with the time and distance from these events that we truly understand the what and whys of life. In retrospect, I was vey disappointed at that time, but looking back, it was a good thing as I showed little promise with my lack of focus and enthusiasm for school at the time.

Later in life, when I joined the military, I had an epiphany and my desire to focus and learn was ignited, and up until the year I retired, I was always eager to learn and strive to succeed with military courses I took.

So, certainly something was amiss all those years ago back in grade three, but later in life it eventually sorted itself out. Sometimes, as parents, we want to protect our kids and want to give them everything and protect them from falling, but perhaps falling isn't so bad if there are lessons to be learned from these experiences. I learned from my own shortcomings, and with my parents' tough decision to hold me back a year, sometimes love and doing the right thing isn't about giving a child everything they want, but rather is about doing what's right for a child, no matter how tough the decision may be.

BIRTHDAY PARTY

RECENTLY, I WAS CELEBRATING A BIRTHDAY AND MY DAUGHTER, Hannah, looked up and asked me, "Daddy, what were birthday parties like when you were a little boy growing up in Cape Breton?" Never one to miss an opening to tell a story about the good old days, I got to explaining to Hannah and her little brother, Reilly, what it was like for me and our childhood parties back when I was their age.

I began by telling them that, growing up in New Waterford during the sixties, birthday parties at that time weren't the big productions and events we make them out to be today. Birthdays during my childhood were not the invitation only events with weeks of planning put into them that are seen now. We had no such things as treat bags for attendees, and certainly no thought of going to a fast food restaurant to host the birthday party. I really don't recall the need for those invited to bring a gift, or if it was even mentioned by our parents to the other parents. If anything, the parties were meant to be a celebration and because money was scarce for all families, gifts were often discouraged. However, if they did bring a gift, they did, and if not, it was never an issue, because it was never about gifts. It was about friends, family, community, and fun.

Very often, birthday parties were an accidental happening. It would all begin with mom saying to me, "Derrick, if you want ask one or two of your friends at school today to come by this weekend, we can have a little party and a birthday cake." Anyone born during this time may remember when teachers would do a little exercise to demonstrate to us kids how rumours would begin. It was a little exercise with one kid whispering a sentence into the persons ear in the front of the first row, and by the time it goes up and down all the aisle to the last person in the last row, it was a different story. Well, this was exactly what happened, when I asked one person to come to my home on the weekend for a little party we were having. I told a couple of the guys I played with from my class, that we were having hot dogs and a birthday cake on Monday at school and then by Friday, the whole class was somehow invited and I didn't understand how this could have happened, I only told two guys, really!

With my birthday being in early October, as the day arrived, there were usually lots of leaves on the ground in front of our house underneath the two white birch trees. Dad would have the leaves piled up, and we would be out in the front yard playing in the leaf pile, and as people slowly began to arrive, and the group became larger and larger, we would run, play games, and anticipate the start of the party. Mom would be in the kitchen boiling some hot dogs and mixing Kool-Aid, getting ready for what she thought were just four or five of my friends.

Dad had gone up to Buddy Graham's store to pick up my birthday cake they had ordered a few days earlier, later when he returned home and walked down the sidewalk to the house, he looked around at the crowd that had gathered shaking his head.

By the time we all piled into the house, there were almost thirty of us. It was a full house, and once mom realized that I had invited to many kids to the house, she never panicked. She just sent dad back up to the store to get more hot dogs and buns and a couple of bottles of pop. Lucky for us, we had my Aunt, Mary Jane, there helping, who was joking with us kids all throughout the party, and she had this high-pitched, infectious laugh that would have everyone laughing along with her.

Looking back at those times, birthday parties were more about neighbourhood kids, playing games and singing. Of course, with much anticipation these times were also about blowing out of the candles, making a wish with finally the eating of the birthday cake by everyone. Later in the evening, once all the kids had left, there was eventually opening the gifts mom and dad had bought for me. More than anything I remember about that day, it was about having fun with my friends and being a kid.

SPRING RAIN

TODAY, AS ANOTHER THIRTY MILLIMETRES OF SPRING RAIN IS falling here at my home in Pembroke, I think it's been a little too much this time of year, so far. But it *is* here, and there's nothing much we can do with mother nature's decisions. I was out for my morning walk already today, and as I walked, I could hear the raindrops tapping on the hood of my jacket, making a familiar rhythm that lulled me back to my Cape Breton childhood.

Walking along, my mind was brought back to those times as a kid walking to school, the dampness in the cool morning air, the smell of freshness it held. For some reason, I always liked this damp, wet feeling it gave me and perhaps that's why I did so well as a soldier during my career. As I continued with my walk, I was taken back to those times of walking along the Heelan Street sidewalk and memories of spring crocuses and bright-green grass, still awaiting its first cutting of the season, with the clouds above unleashing their nourishing rain.

I recall walking to school, all the time daydreaming and humming as children do, being one with my surroundings and taking in the moment. I would occasionally stop along the way to look at the worms as they squirmed around on the sideway after their deep, earthly homes had been flooded, watching the robins taking as many of these worms in their beaks as they could to feed a growing family back in their comfortable tree lofts.

One of my favorite sights was when the Irish brook would flood, as it meandered from the dam up towards the coal mine at Number 12 Colliery making its way to the Atlantic Ocean. We would cut across the field on Second Street and down the hill to the brook. There we would be, a few of the boys, with school still ahead for the day, nevertheless we would challenge one another to a jumping contest. Beginning where the brook was most narrow and continuing to challenge one another with ever more widening parts as we went, with those unable to make the leap falling in getting soaked. We were fearless warriors, oblivious to the clock and the ringing bell, which had just sounded at school. Later, we would arrive at St. Agnes, late and soaked with the brown water from the brook, smelling of wet pit rats and green pond scum. I'm sure we were a treat for our teachers.

Then, of course, there would be the end of the day walk home. It would still be raining out, and though almost dry from our earlier adventures, we would have at it again, playing and splashing with the water running down our faces, trying to top each other jumping the brook. I recall getting home and putting my books on the veranda. I'd stay outside with Kim and Andrea, and we would get soaked to the skin, taking off our shoes and running around the wet grass as it tickled our toes. There wasn't the thought of going inside at all. We were free, enjoying the pleasure of the moment, playing in the rain. Once we were fully soaked from running in the puddles and dripping with rainwater, we would go into the house and then get washed dried off and put on warm clothes. By then, Mom would have supper on, and we felt revitalized with an energy I could never explain.

It was during these times of my childhood where every little boy built some type of cabin in the back yard, and I was no exception. In my back yard was a little cabin on the corner of our property, with the Quigley's house to the back, and the Stanford's to the side. I recall sitting there in a cold, damp rain, a small candle for light that danced in the quiet of the moment to the sound of the rain tapping on the tin roof. There was nothing better than a little bit of time alone with myself outside, I always found it good for my soul.

The rain would eventually stop, and the dampness clear up. The next morning, I noticed the dewdrops on the flowers as we walked to school; they looked like diamonds as they shone in the sunlight of early morning. Small, purple flowers mixed in with the clover would pop up on all the lawns along the way. A rainbow would appear in the distance, and dreams of a pot of gold would enter our minds, only to be interrupted by a droplet of water gently touching our heads, as it fell off the overhanging leaves on the branches along the sideways where we walked. In the distance, a lawnmower could be heard doing its early morning work, followed by the smell of fresh cut grass which brought a newness to the day.

As we grow older, we seemingly forget to enjoy ourselves in these moments. We become hardened with the weighty issues of adulthood and forget even the most innocent and sweet of childhood memories. Of course, we cannot stay children forever, but we should never forget the joyful and playful selves we used to be, those sweet, innocent moments of pure delight and enjoyment.

We need to occasionally remind ourselves to enjoy the rain, to go out and get soaked, refresh those memories. We live in a time where we forget who we are, forget to enjoy ourselves, forget what love is, and lose ourselves to the adult pressures and things of life. As children, we make these innocent and beautifully elegant choices to walk in the rain, to play street hockey or throw a ball back and forth to one another. As adults, we become focused on mortgage, money, and adult things, we forget to look for the fun things all around us, which are free and keep us healthy. Even children of today don't enjoy these same experiences with the same intensity as we did, and it saddens me.

So, today I wanted to walk in the rain and soak it all in, so to speak, go back to that time that was, and wish for all the raindrops of the past to return and wash away all the weighty thoughts of adulthood and, for a moment, allow the raindrops to bring me back to that time. I allowed myself to get soaked today, and it was worth it. Go grab your umbrella, and go outside for a walk. Enjoy the free things around you, which heal your mind and soul. Be a kid again, if for only a moment.

Despite growing up and becoming an adult, I still try to fight it occasionally. Times such as today, where I had butterflies in my stomach, a freshness and newness like a nervous first date, when your stomach quivers with excitement and anticipation. I do miss those times of jumping the brook, running around in the front yard in my sock feet getting soaked, then getting dry and having mom giving us a warm cup of soup. So today, I stole some time, went back, and got soaked, under the rain and drizzle, thoughts of childhood once again flooding my mind, and for a moment, I was walking down Heelan Street to school without a care in the World.

CHRISTMAS IN NEW WATERFORD

CAN REMEMBER THE 1973 CHRISTMAS SEASON, I WAS ONLY TWELVE years old and didn't fully understand or appreciate everything the town of New Waterford had gone through during that difficult year. With the 12 Colliery Mine fire and subsequent closure, the miners were out of work and receiving very little money from unemployment, it was shaping up to be a difficult year for the entire town. There were a few arguments between mom and dad that wafted upstairs to our little ears about money, we were supposed to have been asleep when they were downstairs talking. I could hear mom saying to my father "Where are we going to get money to pay the bills Freddie, to buy gifts and food for the kids at Christmas?" Even as a child, I could feel the strain and stress they were dealing with and I suspect this was a conversation throughout many homes around town at the time.

However, even though they had this hardship to face, still they pushed forward and tried to make Christmas have meaning for us. For mom it was a month-long marathon, and for the family, she was the driving spirit that made this time so special. She hung the garland from the ceiling, and as the Christmas cards arrived in the mail, strung them along the threshold of the living room, making it come alive with welcoming notes, letters, and cards from friends and relatives, both near and far. There were candy and nuts placed on the tables in the living room, and plastic Santa's on the tables.

I remember dad, with Kim and I, driving out to an area behind New Waterford Lake for our yearly Christmas tree. Dad grew up in New Victoria and said that the best Christmas trees in all of Cape Breton were there. We hopped into the car, a Mercury Meteor Montcalm, and drove out to the tracks off Daley Road and began to walk towards the lake. I'm sure it was only a half hour or so, but in my child's mind, it might as well have been forever as we walked in the deep snow with my toes and feet beginning to tingle with the cold, I wanted to go home but dad kept moving forward on a mission to find just the right tree. This had been where dad was brought up, and he knew these woods like the back of his hand, where to go to find that perfect tree, but I didn't understand or care at the time as I was getting colder and more uncomfortable with every step we took. However, it wasn't too long when dad found the biggest and most beautiful fir tree I had ever seen, it was in the woods standing with the other trees, standing out as if a light was above it as in some angelic finding, standing there glowing most perfectly. Dad then took the bucksaw and in no time, he cut it down and dragged it all the way back to the car. Putting it on the roof and tying it down we finally headed home. In the end dad was right about the tree, and eventually as my toes and feet thawed out it seemingly wasn't that big of a deal. As I reflect on this memory, I am still impressed with the skills and knowledge my father had in finding that Christmas tree and of how perfect it was.

Once we got home, dad placed it in the living room, tying it to the wall so it wouldn't fall. He would then fill the bucket up with water and a couple of cups of sugar, which was the way they would feed the tree while it was indoors for the holidays. The smell and feel of the fir tree was amazing, and it meant to us children that Christmas was only a couple of days away. Once the tree was secured, mom took over and layered on the lights, the kind where if one went out the entire set would go out, and then it would be testing each of the painted lights until the burnt out one was found. I remember the smell of the paint on these lights as they heated up. Next were the ornaments, then garland and icicles, and finally, with a can of snow spray a good dosing of snow to complete the Christmas tree.

With only a day or two remaining in school before the Christmas holidays it was time to exchange gifts, we had drawn names from a box a week or so earlier and were supposed to keep them a secret from each other and only to put the persons name on the gift, what I now know as a Secret Santa and we were told the gifts were to be no more than two dollars. The day after the Christmas concert, when we went to school for our last day before the break, we gave and received our classroom gifts. That year I had received the Life Savers Book with 8 rolls of different flavours.

When the holidays began, we stayed up later at night, after a hard day of playing outside, and watched all the Christmas shows we could. *The Charlie Brown Christmas Special, Rudolf the Red Nosed Reindeer* in Claymation, *Dr. Seuss' The Grinch that Stole Christmas*. I would also watch some of the old black and white movies, such as *Holiday Inn* with Bing Crosby and Fred Astaire, or *Miracle on 34th Street*. I still watch these today with my own children. Dad always wanted to watch the Montreal Canadians, he was a Canadians fan, through and through.

On Christmas eve mom, put on a small turkey and ham as we readied for midnight mass at St. Agnes. I remember going into the church; it felt so welcoming, with the choir was singing Christmas songs a half hour prior to Mass beginning. On this Christmas Eve, it was Father Michael MacSween, and he was as always funny and pleasant to listen to. A bonus with Father MacSween as well was that he didn't like a long Homily, so Mass was always a little more economical with him than with any of the other Priests.

After Mass, we walked home in the cool Winters air with a fresh snowfall just beginning. As we walked, we held our parent's hands laughing and giggling along the way trying to catch snowflakes on our tongues as they tickled our faces. Finally arriving home, we entered the house where we were greeted to the welcoming smell of turkey, ham, and potatoes and sweets. After a small midnight meal, we were then sent off to bed so "Santa" would come. Because of the fire this year at Number 12 Colliery, we knew that gifts were going to be few that year due to money being tight with the coal mines shut down. But no matter—we were a family, we were together for Christmas, that was all that mattered.

When we awoke the next morning, and ran downstairs, there was one gift for each of us. Kim got an electric race car set, the kind where the cars had the wires on the bottom, and where they contacted the metal strips on the track, then they would zoom around as you pressed the toggle. Andrea got a doll and dollhouse, and I got a small, blue typewriter. There were also a few pair of socks and a shirt, and this was what we got. We were happy, we had no real expectations of big or expensive gifts, whatever we got for Christmas we knew it was what mom and dad could afford. The most important thing was we realized how much they sacrificed for us, most coal miners families during this time had little. We were all in similar circumstances, in the same boat and we accepted this, just enjoying one another's company, the music, and visiting each others' homes, with no expectations and no big needs.

Looking back at Christmas seasons before and after 1973, many memories are now fading, but I do remember that every year our parents would give up their own wants and needs for us and most often do without. But what I remember most was family, no distractions, no computers, iPads or iPhones, no TV or outside World distractions, only the record player or radio playing Christmas music, and us as a family, with no care in the world. Time was frozen for that moment. Mom and dad laughing and watching us enjoy our gifts in the comfort of a loving home.

These memories are the best gifts I have from my parents from this time. I find myself now telling my own two children about my childhood, my thoughts on how much harder it was than theirs is nowadays, but this is all relevant to when your born, isn't it? When I look back at these times, it was the wonderment of that first snowfall, a chance to use that new sled and playing all day coming home cold, wet, and happy, mom having some cookies and hot chocolate ready. The gift of Christmas is family, not physical gifts, and these memories I have in my heart still light up my imagination every Christmas season, causing a tear to come to my eye with what I had back then and what I have now with my own family.

CLAPPING
CHALKBOARD ERASERS

REMEMBER ST. AGNES ELEMENTARY SCHOOL AND EVERYTHING THAT school was back then. There was the fresh scent of a clean hallway that school janitor, Mr. Ray McLean, had just done the night before, the sweet smell of the pencil shavings, crayons, and the strong smell of printing ink from the handouts we got, the ones where the teacher had written on carbon paper and then made copies using the mimeograph machine.

I was recently at my children's school for family night, and there were games in every classroom. As we went around to all sixteen classes, the one thing I couldn't help but notice was the slow death of the traditional chalkboard. Every classroom in the school now had smart boards and projection screens. The fronts of the classes were now armed with iPads and four-foot TV screens. A few classes still had the old, black chalkboards, but they were buried under the technology like dinosaur fossils, and that familiar chalky dust smell I had grow up with was no longer present in the classes.

In this age of environmentalism, I think perhaps we need to go retro in some respects, see the conservation that was in use when I was growing up, a time when grocery stores used paper bags and boxes for packing. When I think of it, what was more recyclable and reusable than the good, old-fashioned chalkboard? I remember every Friday afternoon as the day was ending, an hour or so before last bell the routine would begin, it was time for the end-of-week cleanup so the class would be ready for Monday morning. There was the washing of the chalkboards, picking up of old papers and tests from people's desks, and straightening out the hallway hangers where we placed out coats and boots. But the most anticipated task be called out was to go and "clap" the chalkboard erasers. Boy, it felt special as Mrs. Oliver would pick two different kids every Friday to take the erasers out and clap them.

One week, I was picked along with another boy, and we had to go to the side wall outside on the gym wall. Then it would begin, we would have fun tapping out our names, making designs, and occasionally trying to draw a picture all over the wall while clapping them against the wall. Sometimes it would get silly, and we would tap each other on the backside or on the arm or head, and then a good, old-fashioned chalkboard eraser fight would break out. We would laugh and laugh as hard as we could, as we ran around hitting one another, and then eventually would return to class covered with chalk. Mrs. Oliver would look over her glasses with a stern look on her face and say something sarcastic, but she had this half smile behind it all. There would be dust everywhere, on the walls, the ground, on our clothes, on our faces, up our noses and in our ears and in our hair. It was glorious to be out there on a Friday afternoon, clapping the erasers. It was never punishment or work, always fun.

The teachers would have us go to the mimeograph machine and spend a half hour wearing out our arms, turning out copies of handouts for the next weeks assignments, while another student would cut them on the big cutting board, while another would staple. Maybe it was the act of clapping the brushes and being a part of maintaining your classroom that made the whole experience special, I'm not sure, but whatever it was, we were always active in helping our teacher, and why not? There was a civic pride in the classroom. It was never felt like work or a punishment to do any of these jobs. We were made to feel special. We were contributing in our own small way to the group, helping the teacher by doing these simple but essential tasks, which otherwise she would have to do herself.

Unfortunately, my own children will never experience this active participation in their education. In their current school, and I imagine in most modern elementary schools, all classrooms have smart boards, projectors, and dry erase boards. Unlike my generation, today's children have perhaps become more passive participants, consumers of education.

Perhaps many of today's problems with children's education, with bullying, with loners, is that we are too worried about giving them all the advantages of modern technology and the life that we didn't have, all at the expense of having the freedom to make their own mistakes and learn to negotiate as problems arise through their school years. It is we adults who are the problem, by not allowing todays children to experience independence and make decisions at a child's level and be allowed to make their own mistakes, learning from them without a parental safety net. Maybe, just maybe, we are forgetting the basics of children's play and of just being a kid out there by the gym on a Friday afternoon, clapping the erasers and having dusty fun.

COAL DELIVERY

WHEN I WAS A CHILD ALMOST EVERY HOME IN NEW Waterford, as well as most of Cape Breton for that matter, was heated with coal. Some homes even had two or three types of stoves in them. There was a coal fired oven for cooking and heat in every kitchen. Many homes had pot belly heating stoves in their living rooms, and very often in the basement would be a coal-fired boiler, which heated the water for the wall radiators. As fall would approach, mom would put in a call to the local coal chute up on King Street, to order coal. The coal chute was located between 10th Street, King Street, and Wilson Avenue. I still remember walking by there as a kid and wondering why was it located in the middle of town. Right in the middle of town were these coal chutes, train tracks cutting the town in half all the way from the old Number 14 and 16 Colliery's. There were usually five coal cars elevated high atop the trestles, with the high banks of earth on either side of it. The area itself was surrounded by a 10-foot-high chain link wire fence with barbed wire on the top, keeping us kids out. Some of the neighbourhood kids would use the hills outside the chutes during the winter for sliding, as this was one of the highest points around the Mount Carmel area, and you could have a good long run down the hill.

In the middle of the coal yard was a small building, where the men in their coal trucks would go get the delivery orders and record the trips they made. As the calls came in from around town, the trucks would back into the areas below the chutes, then coal would then be released from the chutes into the trucks, for home delivery. They Coalmen would release one tonne of coal, or about 2000 pounds, at a time. Once the truck arrived at a home, they would back in and set up a wooden guide by what was a designated coal window in the basement foundation. I remember that these men were stocky, short, and powerful, wide at the shoulders with strong muscular backs and large forearms. The two Coalmen would use pan shovels to unload the truck, these shovels had a short handle for powerful strokes and the scoop was an oversized steel blade to unload the coal in a fast and efficient manner.

Once the door to the basement chute was opened, together they would set to work, putting their heads down and began working in rhythm back and forth each taking their turn to throw a shovel of coal into the chute. As they were swinging their shovels I remember the rhythmical sounds of the coal rolling off the shovel as each took turns, "cling, clang, cling, clang" they would take turns back and forth, until the back of the truck would be emptied in only a few minutes. Then being the professionals, they were when completing the task, they would remove the coal guide going into the basement, clean up the coal which may have fallen around the window and shovel this remaining coal into the basement. Once they collected their money it was off to the coal yards to pick up another load and off to the next house for delivery. It was that simple.

There were some basements that had hoppers, where the peat coal would be automatically fed into the furnace, saving the need to go down and fill up the furnace and stoke it every day. However, most basements in those days contained a coal corral, as was the case in our home. As a little boy, I had to go into the basement to get a bucket of coal every morning as the day began, and then again later at night before bed. From November to the end of March, you didn't want to be the first one out of bed when we coal was used. I'm not too sure about other homes, but in ours, the unwritten rule was that the first one up had to light the kitchen stove.

I remember waking up early one morning and needing to use the bathroom so bad, but praying that someone was already awake. Sticking my head out from under the blankets, I could see my breath in the cold morning air of my bedroom. On seeing this, I knew dad was still at work and no one else had been up yet to light the stove. I waited, then waited a little longer to hear if mom would get up before me, or perhaps my brother Kim. It was a little game everyone played, because no one wanted the work associated with the starting the fire. But it wasn't going to happen; my bladder wouldn't let it. My desperate need to pee over-rode the need to stay warm, and I could not hold out any longer. Once up, I quickly dressed and got ready to head downstairs to get the fire ready, but first I had to attend to other urgent matters.

Now, the lighting of the kitchen stove was a semi-religious experience, with the full, ceremonial rituals surrounding its lighting that any Mass may have contained. The first thing I would have to do was to shake the stove grates, removing the old ashes and cinders from the night before. Then, I had to slide out the metal box in the bottom of the stove and take the ashes outside to the backyard and dump them out on the ash pile. Almost everyone in town had an ash pile in the backyard, which would be used over the winter to deposit the ashes until they could be hauled away in the spring, when a local haulage truck would be hired to take them to the dump. Others in the neighbourhood took the ashes and spread them over their driveways to have a better grip for the car tires and fill in ruts. On returning after emptying the ashes in the backyard, I would go back into the kitchen, slide the ash box back and open the top of the stove, preparing it for the fire. Before this, I would have to take the empty coal bucket down to the basement and fill it.

Preparing the fire consisted of placing old newspaper in the bottom, on top of the grates. Then, on top of these papers, smaller pieces of kindling would be added, and then the fire lit. Once the starter wood caught fire, you'd add a small shovel of coal, then you would check after a few moments to make sure it had caught. When you opened the stove top to look inside, a little puff of smoke would escape and go into the air above the stove, with this escaping smoke you would smell the carbon from the coal as it burnt. You would then add another scoop of coal and then another, until it was caught and going good. That was it. Once it was going, all you had to do was once in awhile stoke it up, shake the grates, and add a small shovel of coal every now and then to keep the house warm all day and into the evening.

The amusing thing now in looking back at these times was, once the house was warmed up, everyone came crawling out of the woodwork.

Seemingly fully awake for the day in a nice warm house, pretending to be oblivious to the torture I had just endured getting the stove ready, but I guess that was the price of having a small bladder in a cold house.

TRADING
COMIC BOOKS

WHEN I WAS A LITTLE KID, ROUGHLY SIX OR SEVEN YEARS OLD, I started to get interested in reading comic books. It all began with reading the ones that were very simple and had a little moral at the conclusion and which children would understand, comics such as *Casper the Friendly Ghost* or *Richie Rich*. I think it was the simplicity of these comics and the moral lessons within these stories that were easy to understand and to adopt. Usually, they were about helping one another, or helping a stranger, avoiding the bad things life puts before us, or other things such as this.

One of my fondest memories was when I would go up to the corner store for mom or one of the neighbours. I would run up to Buddy Graham's Dairy and buy a copy of *Casper*, *Wendy the Good Little Witch*, or *Richie Rich*. I would go over to the tall, merry-go-round comic rack, which was over by the regular magazine racks. I would pick up a comic and start losing myself for what seemed forever, but it was only a few moments before the store clerk, Emma, would say, "Hey, this isn't a library is it?" I would catch myself and close the book. Taking it up to the counter, I would put my little hand into my pocket, taking out the thirteen cents for the comic, buy it and take it home to finish reading it.

The next thing for me in my reading development was The Big Little Books, which were fantastic and seemingly fit just right in our little hands. There was nothing better than holding one of these as you read. They seemed so big, yet so small. I remember getting my first one and being so excited when Mom gave it to me. It was Popeye and his girlfriend Olive Oil. I read that first one over and over for the longest time. I liked the Big Little Books so much that I still have a few, which I have then passed onto my children, who have also since enjoyed them repeatedly. These were the ones with Bugs Bunny, Woody Woodpecker, and Popeye, as well as the more serious ones such as Flipper and Rat Patrol. Even now, when I pick them up, the memories that were created around them as a child come rushing back, bringing a smile to my face.

As I grew older, I would have a change in taste and move onto comics such as *The Fantastic Four, Batman and Robin, The Flash, Green Lantern,* and so many more. This was the beginning of raising my awareness of good versus bad, as was the case with Batman versus the Riddler.

I enjoyed the *Archie and His Gang* comics. These seemed to be a blueprint for how to act, or not to act, as a teenager. Some of the boys liked Veronica, because she came from a wealthy family and was a bit stuck up, while others liked Betty, because she was more down to earth and came from a humbler upbringing than her archrival, Veronica. I kind of liked Jughead, mostly because he wasn't really interested in the girls, he was more so into eating, especially hamburgers.

I still recall jumping the fence from my backyard into the Quigley's yard and heading down to West Avenue. Every few weeks, the topic of trading comics would come up, and we would agree to meet at one of our homes and take out pile of comics there to sit and trade. Most often we would meet at Christopher's home, usually it would be Chris, Bobby and myself, each of us with our little stack of gently read comic books, sitting on the floor, ready to do some serious trading. It was always fun, and we would just sit there for hours and hours, sometimes reading each others' comics from front to back before trading, only to take them home to read them once again, they never got boring.

My taste in comics as a teenager, in retrospect, foreshadowed my eventual career choice. I began reading *Sgt. Rock* and liked the stories these comics contained. Most of the storylines were from World War II and seemed much more realistic than those I had read earlier. The actions of Sgt. Rock were more achievable, something that I could do. I would never be Batman or Superman, but could be a soldier and take care of others so later in life. Eventually, I would join the military and be a soldier, a medic to be exact. Probably not as cool as Sgt. Rock, but I still tried to be the best soldier I could while overseas representing Canada.

As I grew older, so did my tastes in comics once again, and I moved into the Dell Comics, which were more about transitioning from teenage years to adulthood, with subjects such as Horror, Sci-fi, and these more adult-like comics would come out a year or so prior to the movies. Then, of course, who didn't read the *Mad* comic books every month when they came out. I guess these were my first social commentary or political satire books. They were certainly different from anything I had ever read up to that point. I never lost my taste for the *Mad* comics and their brand of satire, and I especially enjoyed the "Spy Vs. Spy" series.

Recently, I came across a small box in the basement. It was all taped up, with COMICS written across the top of it. I took the tape off and found about twenty-five *Sgt. Rock* comic books. Wow, was I ever excited to find these! Immediately, I thought of those times with Bobby and Chris trading comic books. I realize that I am middle aged now, but for those few moments after finding those Sgt Rock Comics, for a moment I was once again a kid sitting on the kitchen floor, trading comics with Chris, Bobby. All of us with our little pile of comic books, laughing, talking, and telling each other all about the stories we had read.

DON'T SLEEP OVER AT DERRICK'S HOUSE

I WAS ABOUT ELEVEN YEARS OLD AND FULL OF BADNESS WITH A LITTLE tinge of evil, always getting my father going and picking on him until he would lose his temper with me. There was this one night I remember, in the summer of 1972 when we were out all day, playing with friends and having fun. We were down at the dam, over in the fields on the other side of the brook, picking blueberries. Once we got a couple of pails full, we took them home, to my place, where mom made us some blueberry muffins and we ate them down while they were hot.

One of the guys I hung out with the most as a kid was Jerome. He was a couple of years older than me, but such a good guy to hang out with. Jerome was easy going and had a gentle personality, he also could play guitar, sing, and tell a funny joke. I asked him if he wanted to sleep over. He said okay, so I asked mom, and she said to us that it would be ok if his mom wouldn't mind. So off we went to Jerome's place to ask his mom if he could sleep over, and she said, "No problem, but remember to mind your manners and listen to Derrick's mom and dad."

He grabbed a t-shirt, pajama bottoms, and his tooth brush, and we were off back to my place, where we had supper then turned on TV, we only had two channels at that time so the pickings were slim. We watched for a little while until Jerome was getting tired, then he asked me where he would be sleeping. When we went upstairs to the bedroom, I pointed to a bed, my bed, and said to take that one. The other, which was my brother Kim's, he was away at camp on Sangaree Island, so I would take his. He wanted to go to bed right then, and as he did, I went back downstairs for a little longer.

Dad was working the night shift and finally got home around 10:30. He was talking to mom, having a coffee. So, I began picking and bugging him, no reason except out of badness I guess looking back. He was slowly losing his patience with me and getting angry when he finally said, "DERRICK, GET TO BED NOW!" So of course, I kept picking and picking, until he finally had enough and took off his belt and started chasing me.

In our downstairs, there were the three rooms joined together with arches, so I was running around and around in circles, with dad in hot pursuit. We must have looked like the Keystone cops. However, he was gaining ground and closing in on me, so I detoured upstairs, sprinting into my bedroom, and diving under my bed, slide to safety from his belt. However, Poor Jerome, who had been quietly asleep in my bed for a couple of hours by then, wouldn't have known or expected what was about to happen. When dad got into the bedroom, it was dark, and he could barely see where I was, he could only see a silhouette in the bed and thought he had me cornered. Huffing and puffing from the chase, he walked over to the bed and said, "Now I got you, you little bugger!"

Dad began whacking Jerome on the arse with the belt, and Jerome was wailing and crying, with my father saying, "Good! you better cry. Now get to bed and stay there." All the time, I was just glad that Jerome had come over that night and took the belt on the arse for me. After dad left the room, Jerome was laying there under the covers on the bed sobbing, and whispered to me, "What did I do? Why is your dad mad at me?"

I didn't know what to say, but also didn't want him to know I was the cause of all this commotion, so I said, "I don't know why Jerome, but sometimes dad just shows up and gives us a wack with the belt when he is upset at something we've done earlier in the day. Now, you better be quiet or he'll be coming back in." I lied and at the time it sounded like a good explanation to me as it was falling from my lips, eventually Jerome calmed down and stopped crying, so I went to my brother's bed and crawled in, and we both slept until the next morning.

The next day, Jerome didn't want breakfast or anything that came with the possibility that he might encounter my dad again, he just wanted to get out of the house. However, when we went downstairs, dad was sitting there in the kitchen, having a coffee and cigarette, giving me dirty looks. Jerome was behind me and from his vantage point, he thought dad was looking at him and at that point he wanted to get out of the house and back to the safety of his own home. I really think he thought dad was going to chase after him again.

Jerome said a goodbye to my mom and ran all the way home, and I tagged along with him. When he arrived home, he burst into tears, telling his mother of the terrible night he had sleeping over at my house, telling her that Freddie Nearing gave him the belt. Suddenly in an angry voice, Jerome's mom said "What? Why would he do that?" Then she took her belt off and wacked his arse a few times herself, saying, "Freddie Nearing is a good man, if he beat you while you were staying at their place, then you must have done something wrong. Why were you acting up at their house, Jerome?"

I felt bad, because poor Jerome got it again, and never had done anything in the first place. But I didn't want to say anything about it being my fault. But I couldn't hide away much longer from the truth. Then, his mom decided to come down to my house with Jerome and I to speak with my parents about what had happened the night before. She began by telling them that she was so sorry if Jerome was acting up last night when he slept over, and it would never happen again. She said she understood giving him a couple of belts in the arse, and that she had reinforced this by giving him a couple more once he told her what happened.

Dad and mom turned their head and looked at me. Poor dad was in shock, knowing what he had done, and began to explain and apologize to Jerome's mom, through his embarrassment at what had taken place. I was on the other side of the room and panicking as I knew what was going to take place in a few moments. After she left with Jerome, dad's eyes locked with mine, as he walked to wards me he took his pit belt off and started chasing me around the downstairs, doing the circle from room to room as we did the night before, slowly gaining ground on me, and I once again peeled off, running up to my bedroom. Only this time, he would have the right culprit.

FIRST OF DAY SCHOOL

WOKE UP EARLY ON THAT FIRST MORNING, ANTICIPATING THE BEGIN-ning of the school year as I rolled over in my bed. Looking across the room, my brother bed was empty as Kim was already up. I could smell that the coal stove downstairs was stoked and ready, with mom busy in the kitchen. My baby sister, Andrea, was still in bed. I could hear dad's footsteps as he came to the bottom of the stairs and hollered for me to get up and ready for school. Boy, I was excited for today, my very first day going to school, my first day St. Agnes Elementary and I couldn't wait.

Mom had placed my clothes in the hallway while I was washing, and once I got dressed and ready for the day, there was some toast and jam with a glass of milk waiting for me on the kitchen table. After breakfast, dad told me to come over to where he was sitting and took out his comb and combed my hair, then rubbed my head, telling me to be a good boy for the teacher.

It was a sunny morning that first day at St. Agnes. It was Tuesday, September 6, 1966, and I walked to school with my big brother, Kim. We went down Heelan Street, walking past Finlayson Gas Station and Doughboy's store, then over Irish Brook, heading up Ellsworth Ave passing Cecilia's corner store, next was the barber shop, then the New Waterford Grocery Store, a little up from here we passed Hinchey's Grocery, next to Charlie and Mary Hadley's corner store. Finally, we got to the crosswalk leading up to Convent Street, and we were greeted by the crossing guard, an older gentleman, who held up his sign to have the traffic stop for us as we walked across the street. Then up Convent Street we went, where I was dropped off in front of the school with all the other primary kids by my older brother. As older brothers go, Kim was the best, but being in grade two and in Mrs. MacVarish's class, it wasn't cool for him to be seen with his little brother, so once he told me where to wait, he was like a puff of smoke in the wind and gone!

I stood there for a moment, feeling a bit overwhelmed, while looking up at this seemingly giant building in front of me. It was the three-story elementary school across from St. Agnes Church, and across the parking lot, I could see the big St. Agnes High School, where all the older kids went. I looked up at the St. Agnes Elementary School which was the convent prior to the new one being built. It was gigantic, with ten steps leading up to big, double doors. We would later be told it was the last year for this building to be used as a school. Already, as this new school year was beginning, a newer and smaller school was being constructed, the new St. Agnes Elementary, later to be renamed Frank Angot Elementary, across the street. There was a hand bell rung to start that first day as we lined up in our group and gathered outside, waiting, as all the teachers showed up and called the names of the students in their classes. It was the primary kids to be called first, and I could feel how excited we all were. There were to be two primary classes for this year.

My name was called for the first of the two classes, and once all the names were called, we were told to follow the teacher into the school. On entering the big, double doors at the front of the school, our primary class was immediately to the left. Before I went in my class, I took a moment and looked up the stairs to the second floor; there was a big statue of St. Agnes on a pedestal. The hallway seemed enormous to my little eyes, and the ceiling as high as the sky. Right away, there was a pine smell in the air which would become so familiar to me over the next few years. I imagine this was the case for most kids, during their time in school, it was a pine mixed with crayons and wooden pencils scent that still today reminds me of school. The pine came from the dust bane that was used by the cleaners when they would sweep the floors at the end of each day, but it was the cleanest of smells, and a distinct memory as part of my schooling experience. It was of the consistency of sawdust soaked with pine-sol, and it was used to absorb the dirt and to keep the dust down as the janitors swept the entire school at the end of each day. I learned very early in my life, and through my later years in the military, just how important these people were, and so I always had a special respect for these workers that no one ever seemed to see or acknowledge, but who kept our school always in tip-top shape for us to learn in.

We were told to look for the desk with our name on it. They were the old-fashioned desks, with the ink well and drawer under where you sat, and an armrest to your right. I would later find this to be somewhat difficult with me being left handed, but I adjusted. So here I was, finally, my very first day in school. Once we found our places, we were introduced to our teacher, Mrs. McKay, a very sweet and kind lady who gently got us through those first few days of separation anxiety as we let loose the apron strings of our mothers.

She spoke in a soft voice as she stood in front of the class, and the first order of the day was to sing "Oh Canada," then afterwards say an "Our Father" before doing anything else. Once this was all done, she began to ask each of us our full names. This was awkward for a moment, and would be every year after, it was a time you would hear giggles from the other kids when we would say our full names aloud. My turn came up, and I said, "My name is Derrick Paul Nearing." On hearing my middle name, the others would giggle.

Then, it was a manners and etiquette teaching session, once we had all introduced ourselves. We were taught to speak only when your spoken to, take our turns when speaking, be polite to others, and place your hand up if you want to go the washroom or to ask a question. Then, it was onto the rules; we were told that when someone entered the room, we were to stand up and say, "Good morning, Then, we were taught to bow and curtsy. I think these were all good and important first lessons. We were taught to respect our country with the singing of "Oh Canada," to respect God with the saying of the Lord's Prayer, to respect adults with the group standing up with the greeting of guests, to respect our teacher, as she was there to guide, and finally, to respect one another. These are things that have guided myself all through life, as I headed out to the college, university, and during my thirty-five-year career in the military.

About halfway through the morning, we heard the hand bell once again, and were told this meant morning recess. Then, we were off, running outside to play. The playground was more like a gravel pit, looking back, but at the time, it was all we had, we didn't care as we just wanted to play. There were girls skipping and playing stretch with elastics, seeing how high they could stretch up and over the elastic that was held between two girls. There were the boys playing soccer, catch, or marbles. There were those little boys and girls on the climbing structure. It was a mass of activity, supervised with a playground teacher watching for rough housing or little tiffs that might arise. Then, just like that, it was over, and the bell was rung, and we all went back inside.

When lunchtime came, we all had to run home, since back in the sixties there was no school canteen. We all ran home, retracing the paths we took to get to school, for a quick bowl of soup and a cartoon on TV of Hercules or Fred Flintstone, and then time to head back to school for the afternoon. My brother Kim would have left a few minutes earlier to meet up with his friends, but I would straggle behind and remember when the one o'clock movie would begin, it was called "Midday Matinee" and I usually wanted to stay home and watch it, but mom would send me off to school.

On that first day, Mrs. McKay got down to business, and we began learning how to print the alphabet, and the first letters were to be the smaller case, there were the upper and lower-case letters above the blackboard for examples, I would be looking up at them as I worked trying to be copy them perfectly. She also spoke about consonants and vowels as we learned the alphabet. While busily working, a knock came on the door, and Mrs. McKay answered the door, then she turned around facing us and told us we have a special visitor. She emphasized not to forget what she had taught us in the morning, about how to greet a guest. Then, in came Sister Florence Patrice Nearing, the elementary principle. We all stood up, and we bowed and curtsied and said, "Good afternoon, Sister Florence." She spoke for a few minutes as we sat with our hands folded in front of us quietly, and then a moment later she was gone. Later at recess, everyone in my class asked me if she was my aunt or a relative, but I didn't know her at all before that day, so couldn't give an answer. We finished our alphabet and did a little drawing and art. Then, it was already 3:30 and time to go home.

I think we all felt special that day, and seemingly, all the nervousness and crying that some had with leaving their moms and dads on that first day had now settled, and for these few hours every day in school, Mrs. McKay would become like a second mother to us.

CLOTHESLINE
DRIED CLOTHES

When I was growing up in New Waterford, every house in town had a clothesline in their backyard. It was a simple construction of two poles, a wire rope with a plastic covering over it between them. At times, one of the corners at the back of the house would be used, and still yet, if your mom were a little luckier, she would have the clothesline on a pully system and get to stand in one place while hanging our clothes on the line.

Early every spring, there would be a couple of men going door to door selling cedar clothes line poles. They had peeled the bark off the twelve-foot-long cedar wooden poles, which were whitish in colour, pointed at one end with a V cut out at the other end, for the clothesline to go in between. They would go door to door all over town selling these cedar poles until they were all gone. But this simple innovation kept the clothes from dragging on the grass or ground once the line was burdened with all those wet and soggy clothes.

Mom had the old, bucket wringer-washer out in the back porch. She would push it out and into the kitchen on wash day, hook up the main hose to the water spout and the drain hose into the sink, and then there she would work for the rest of the morning, until the wash was done. There was also a wringer, on the top of the washer and an activator switch to get it rolling, as well as an emergency push bar in case you wanted it to stop the rollers or if clothes became caught in the wringers for some reason. When you hit the emergency push bar, the rollers popped up, releasing them from the gears which turned them, then whatever was caught could be removed. Mom would simply lock it back into place once the obstruction was cleared.

Myself, I was always fascinated with the mechanics of how things worked, always taking things apart and putting them back together to see how they worked. But I was very interested in the whole wringer aspect of the set up and this emergency push bar thing on the top. So, one day, as Mom was in the living room and the agitator was going back and forth, washing the clothes, my brother Kim and I went out to investigate the wringer. There were two rollers that Mom would pull a switch to get them moving, then she would feed the clothes through the two wringers, squeezing all the water out, which would then drain back into the washer.

The clothes would come out the back and only then needed to be put in the clothes basket and hung out on the clothesline. On this one day, my brother Kim and I started the rollers and decided to have a game of chicken. As the rollers were moving, we began with sticking the tips of our fingers into the moving rollers and quickly pulling them out as the skin on the fingertips was being pinched, seeing who was the fastest and bravest. I certainly was neither, as we would soon find out as I took the trophy for the dumbest sibling.

On my last try, my fingers got pulled into the rollers and before you knew, the rollers had me caught up to my knuckles and I was screaming. Kim panicked and ran to get mom, who ran into the kitchen hitting the emergency push bar. It was chaos with everyone running around, chaos for a few minutes. As she pulled my hands out of the roller, they were full of blood from being squeezed between the wringers and pain was shooting all the way from my finger tips to my shoulder. Mom called a taxi and took me up to the New Waterford Consolidated Hospital Emergency Department, where Dr. Nathanson was on duty, so it wasn't too long before I was being seen. I remember Dr. Nathanson looking at the X-Rays and talking to my mom, giving a little chuckle as he told her, "Don't worry Mrs. Nearing, his fingers will be all right. We will just have to cast him for a few weeks until this heals" The damage was done, I had broken three fingers and wrist on my right hand. I was then put into a cast for my right hand and fingers, which took care of the last month of Summer and all sports and playground activities for me until September.

Whoever began this whole washing clothes and hanging them out to dry thing probably didn't know what would evolve from it. From this simple act of washing and cleaning clothes came a whole ritualization of the process. There were the days to do the blankets, days to do pants and shirts, and the days for the undergarments, usually early in the morning. I'm sure people back then would look across the backyards and size up the neighbours' wears as they were hung out to dry. Even in the Olympics of clothes drying, there was stiff competition as to who had the whitest and cleanest. The mothers of that time were like military sergeant majors, as the clothes had to be formed up with blankets, and sheets to the left, towels in the middle, with socks and underwear bringing up the rear... in more ways than one.

Its funny now when I think of how we have been told that our parents and grandparents had wasted so much in "the old days", so much that in modern times we have come up with "green energy" initiatives. I laugh to myself and wonder, when so many municipalities of today have banned the clothesline because of its non-aesthetic look, I think back and wonder "is it todays generations who are really the first green proponents?"

Today I hung out our sheets to dry in our backyard, looking forward to tonight when I go to my bed and pull up the covers to smell the cool fresh aired dried sheets from today's wash. I cannot wait to let the outdoor scent take me back to those times as a child on Heelan Street, all those years ago. Thinking of the hard work mom, and all the moms, must have done back then for us. Closing my eyes, I allow the freshness of the blankets and memories of mom and my Cape Breton home comfort me falling asleep.

FIRST HAIRCUT

GROWING UP IN THE SIXTIES, SHORT HAIR WAS THE NORM FOR boys. I never saw too many boys or older men without a good, old-fashioned brush cut. "Did your haircut come with a bowl of soup," used to be the old saying after a haircut. I still remember my first, tear-filled haircut at Dave Wilkie's Barbershop, when I was around four years old. Prior to this first barbershop haircut, mom would trim it off with scissors and keep it neat. I had lots of blonde curls and she wanted me to have them for as long as I could.

One day, I was up to no good as usual, and somehow got into mom's purse, knowing that this was where she kept her Double mint gum. I took a couple of pieces and slid the silver wrapped gum from its paper sleeve, then removed the shiny wrapper, smelled the wintergreen mint smell, then proceeded to pop them into my mouth, chewing wildly and trying to blow bubbles. At the time, I didn't have any idea of how to blow bubbles, but tried and tried, for the longest time, to get that first bubble, when suddenly, something happened, I finally got one to inflate. Boy, I was so excited as I blew and blew, while it got bigger and bigger, then suddenly, it popped, and the explosion of gum wrapped around my face and into my hair. I panicked and tried to remove it, but the more I tried, the deeper it got into my hair and the worse it got mixed in, until finally, I looked like a ragdoll.

My first thought was that I knew it was wrong going into mom's purse, wrong taking the gum, and wrong for the mess I got myself into. So, not wanting to run and tell mom what I just did, I snuck upstairs to the bathroom. Under the bathroom sink, there was a set of manual hair clippers, so I decided to cut out the hair which had the gum in it. No problem, I thought, just clip the few spots off until the gum was out.

I was sure no one would notice, at least this was what I thought in my four-year-old mind.

I ended up cutting a large patch off the front of my hair, and it was very noticeable as it was right to the skin, with large clumps of hair chopped out. I looked in the mirror and immediately began crying and went downstairs sobbing to mom, she was smiling at me as she held herself back from laughing. She said, "You got yourself into quite the mess this time Derrick, with that big patch of hair missing and the rest with the gum mixed in the hair. It will need to be cut at the barbers."

She asked a couple of the teenage girls in the neighbourhood to take me up to see Dave Wilkie and see what he could do to fix it up. Little did I know what she meant by "fix it up." Here I was, screaming, kicking, and crying as I was dragged up to see the barber by my two escorts, where he put the padded, wooden booster seat on the top of the barber's chair and then went to work as tears rolled down my face. I could see the curls pass my eyes. Watching them fall the same way as I had watched snow falling only a couple of months earlier, causing more tears, screaming, and kicking. I couldn't stop crying. I couldn't figure out why these adults were torturing me this way, the two girls holding me in the chair as Dave cut my hair.

When I got out of the chair, I picked up all my hair off the floor, still crying uncontrollably, and took it all home. I don't know why I took the clippings home, but I was somehow expecting mom to work her motherly magic and make it all better. But that was not to be and mom eventually threw my hair into the garbage. I went upstairs and looked into the mirror once again, I now had white walls on the side of my head where hair use to be. This encounter with Dave Wilkie would be my first, but certainly not last, brush cut.

Later as a teenager, I was downtown one summer night and saw my brother Kim getting into the back of the big army truck which use to pick up the guys in front of Harry Yip's Restaurant. I knew right at once I wanted to join the militia. I went to get all my hair shaved off totally, a "high and tight" military cut all around. I knew Dave liked to do a nice haircut with scissors and the clipper and didn't like to do total brush cuts, but I thought I would ask just this once.

I went up to his barber shop that Saturday and he asked me what I wanted. I told him about the guys in the militia and asked if he could give me a haircut just like them. He shaved the sides off right to the "wood" as they use to say, then clipped the top making it a flat top, then blended it in where the top and sides met. Then, I was ready. At fifteen, I joined the militia. I never looked back, and for thirty-five years I served in the Reserves and Regular forces, looking smart with my smart haircut and uniform on. Later with the Canadian flag on my shoulder, looking clean and well groomed I would eventually be deployed to care for people all over the world.

As I reflect on that time, all those years ago, I am glad now that I got that gum in my hair, got that first haircut and glad that I've kept it high and tight now for well over fifty years. Even to this day I continue this tradition of visiting my barber every Friday, for a little trim and talk of times that were, and of those yet to come.

FIRST SNOW
OF THE YEAR

A FEW WEEKS AGO, WE HAD OUR FIRST SNOWFALL HERE IN THE Ottawa Valley. More of a snow *storm*, with over thirty centimeters falling, and gusting winds for the day after. It had been gusting so badly that school was cancelled for all the valley schools, for today I left the kids in bed. Looking out my front window at seven in the morning, quiet and alone with my thoughts, my childhood memories came flooding back, while the snow danced around the streets with the wind whipping it around making snow drifts. Later in the morning, when I went outside to shovel the driveway, I got a whiff of the fresh, cold air and newness that first snow of the year had brought.

I believe what still excites all of us on an occasional snow day, when everything is shut down, is that these times force us to slow everything down, in today's hectic, modern, fast-paced, computer-driven life. I find these days of silence take me back to my youth, to times when things were slower, without the pressure today's kids have with being continuously connected and the pace of today's world. Nature forces us to shut our minds down, as stores, schools, and streets are all closed, creating and an unexpected but delightful change to our day-in-and-day-out rituals. It allows us to recharge our imaginations, to reconnect with nature and with one another.

The snows of my childhood on Heelan Street were much, much deeper than those of today, seemingly up to the roof, in my mind's eye. Dad would shovel the snow so high that, going down the sidewalk into the house, seemed as if we were walking through a tunnel. I remember one time, dad decided to take my brother Kim and I over to the washhouse at No. 12 Colliery, so we could shower during the beginning of an innocent looking snowfall. Suddenly, halfway there, as we got to the walkway over the brook at the bottom of West Ave, the wind picked up and snow began to fall faster, hitting our faces, me squeezing dad's hand so tight and thinking the wind would pick me up and carry me away, as my breath was being taking away. I think dad dragged me by my arm most of the way from the brook to the washhouse. Once we were inside the big doors, the heat from the boiler hit us, I knew we were safe, at least until it was time to go back home.

My favourite activity was sledding. We would go on a little hill behind MacDonald's Hardware, which was up the street from our home and it was here we used as our sledding spot, and take a run and hop on our sleds and go down Mary Avenue towards Heelan Street. I had a single rider sled and loved this old thing so much as used it until it eventually wore out. Other kids had nicer, faster, bigger sleds and toboggans, but it didn't matter; this one was mine. When we went sliding, there was the initial drop from the top of the little hill from behind MacDonalds's Hardware to Mary Avenue and hitting the ditch, hard, before finally getting up to a good speed going down the hill. We would sled for hours at a time, into late in the evening, then make our ways home, cold, wet, and rosy cheeked with satisfaction.

The first heavy snowfall also meant the first snowball fight of the year would take place, this would ensue and carry on if there was good sticky snow to make the snowballs. We usually built a snow fort first, then someone would throw a first snowball and then it was game on. We would be trying to make and throw snowballs as fast as possible on each side of the fort with a couple of the boys making them non-stop, while the others threw, then occasionally switching roles. Of course, there would ultimately be one of us hit with a snowball to the face, then we would all stop in our tracks, with the one who was hit crying holding his face and run off to their home. Immediately, we would quickly break up the snowball fight and all run off, not knowing who was going to get into trouble. Eventually, we would all get a snowball in the face at one time during the winter, and everyone eventually got the "you're going to blind someone" lecture at home from our parents.

The next day, we couldn't wait to get out to the fort again. As with any of our seasonal activities, we stopped only long enough to go home, throw our gloves and toques on the register or in front of the kitchen stove, and eat and warm up a little. Mom would tell me that if I stayed out too long, I would lose my toes and ears to frostbite, so we were bundled up, which took some time. And by the time we got dressed, of course, I would need a pee, and undress, and go through the whole procedure once again. But these were the rites of passage, stories to be told and retold.

In the end, I guess the magic in that first snow of last week was in just looking out on a quiet moment and seeing the footprints left behind from the black capped chickadees, as they hopped across the freshly fallen snow. Inhaling that cool air, and the freshness of its newness, and squinting your eyes with the brightness from the blanket of white in the morning sun, seemingly clearing the mind of worries.

DOESN'T HE LOOK GOOD?

M Y DAD USED TO SIT AT THE KITCHEN TABLE EVERY DAY around supper time, reading the *Cape Breton Post*. Like many of his time, he always began at the front of the paper, with reading the obituaries. Back in those times, the obituaries were the first things when you opened the Post, everyone would look and see who had passed. I used to joke with dad and tell them I saw them as employment ads, because when someone would pass away their job would need to be filled, he wasn't amused with my jokes. As he read, occasionally he would see someone's name from town he knew who had died, then, he would tell Mom, "Patsy, send Derrick to see Patty and Gertie Copley down the street for a couple of Mass cards." So, with this instruction, off I would be sent with $5.00 to purchase a couple of Mass cards.

Patty would call out to his wife, "Gertie!! someone's here for Mass cards!" Then, she would come to the front door with her big smile and say," Come in, Derrick. And so, is this for Mr., *So-and-so?*" She would write his name inside them, taking the money from me, she would then write the persons name on the card, pass them to me and with this I would run back home with the cards.

My dad would wash and shave, put on his best, and head down by himself to McGillivray's funeral home. Once there, they would always ask him, "Hey Freddie, how are you doing?" and "What shift are you on this week?" The usual miners' small talk they all had in common.

Once, when I was around sixteen years old, Dad and I were sitting in the kitchen. He had just returned form one of his friend's funerals, and I got to asking him, "Dad, why do you feel you have to go to every funeral in town?" Sipping on his coffee, he looked over and began to explain to me why he attended funerals all the time, even of those of people he wasn't even that close to. He said, "Derrick, first, attending funerals shows that you care. The family may not even know you only worked with the fellow who had passed, but they are in pain, and everyone they see, they believe was their fathers friend. It's about caring and being there for the family. It really doesn't matter that you only knew them a little at work, the family wants to know he was loved, and he meant something to others. This is it, and it's the least we can do for them."

Then, I asked him, "What do you say to someone when you go to a funeral, Dad?" He told me that sometimes he doesn't say a word. It's just the fact that he took the time and attended, and he can feel that the people are comforted, words unnecessary. Perhaps the shake of a hand, a pat on a back, or the comfort of a hug. "It is about being there with them, Derrick. And should you feel sad, that's okay, because they are hurting, and cry, because they will miss their loved one. If you have nothing to say and are stuck for words, just say, 'Sorry for your troubles.' That's all you need to say; they will understand." I have used this advice many times during my life.

He went on to explain to me that, no matter who they were, whether a good friend or just an acquaintance, they were important to their family, to the coal mining community, to New Waterford. They could have been the worst SOB ever, but to the family, they were the best, and this funeral is a send off for that loved one, the last opportunity for a family to remember them, with everyone from the community attending the funeral. He went on to tell me, "The family will always remember you attended. That's what's important: the family, and their saying good bye to a loved one. Your being there is all that matters. In the weeks and months to follow, they will look at the tags on the flowers, all the signatures in the book of condolences, all those Mass cards, and be comforted. All just because you were thoughtful enough to attend."

Then he told me, "I got more life behind me than in front, and a friend's funeral makes you appreciate what you have had up to this point. Make the most of the time in front of you, Derrick!" Dad gave me very good advice that day.

Finally, he told me with a chuckle, "Derrick, if I don't go to everyone's funeral now, who's going to come to mine?" He went on to tell me when his time comes, and he is down at McGillivray's being waked, not to let people look at him in the coffin and say, 'Your dad looks good, Derrick.' Dad would say, "How the hell can you look good when your dead? I never understood when people said this at a funeral."

When Dad passed on March 17, 1982, the line up began at the funeral home, and people walked by his coffin, knelt, said a prayer, then shook our hands, or patted me on the back. Many hugs were given, so many hugs. There were a couple of people who said, "Derrick, doesn't your dad look good?" and I smiled hearing this and remembered dad's words, "If I don't go to their funeral, who will come to mine?

So, as I write this, tomorrow I will be going to a funeral here in Petawawa. It's for a soldier who was a friend of mine. I do not know his wife, his mom, dad, brothers, and sisters, but I do remember what Dad told me all those years ago. They will always remember that I attended, that he was loved. And that's what's important. That's all that matters.

HAND-ME-DOWNS

I WAS BORN AT THE TAIL END OF THE BABY BOOM, A TIME OF BIG families and lots of siblings, but being in a coal miners family there was not a lot of money. Being brought up in a family of seven and growing up on Heelan Street, I was unaware of just how little we all had. Most families in those days had only their father working, with the moms at home managing the house, with only the husband's menial wages coming in. To be sure, life was occasionally tough as we had to share as a community. Although we never had much, by way of material things, as an adult I realize that by bring born the time I was, we had it all.

There were a couple of families around the neighbourhood with eight to ten kids. During this time, there weren't the Value Village or Salvation Army thrift stores we see now. There was a chain called Frenchie's, but overwhelmingly, the way of passing on clothes was the sharing through hand-me-downs from neighbour to neighbour. I still remember those times when neighbours would bring a bag full of clothes and say to mom, "Here, Patsy. The boys are finished with these. See what Kim and Derrick can use, then pass the rest on." It was done in a matter of fact way, never demeaning, or condescending. It was just the way it was back then. We would then patiently wait until the neighbour left, at which point there would be an explosion of clothes, as we ripped open the bag to try on the t-shirts, pants, and sneakers.

Some clothes would be too big, which was good, because you could grow into them, while others would be too small and look like flood pants. There would be pants too loose at the waist, and others you needed to take a deep breath in before tightening. But overall, there were more than enough clothes for Kim and me, and so we would take them upstairs to our bedroom and put them away. Once in our rooms, we would take our old clothes from the closets and drawers and place these into a garbage bag for mom to pass on to some other neighbours, with small kids, repeating the chain of hand- me-downs as had been done for us.

I remember one Winter we had gotten a few bags of clothes and when I opened the first bag and took out the pants, shorts, and sweaters, slowly as I got deeper into the bag there was to my astonishment a pair of skates. They were the old type tube skates and I couldn't wait to try them on, and when I did, to my amazement, they fit perfectly. I had never skated before and saw the other kids in the neighbourhood skate at St Agnes, or in their backyard rinks, and I wanted to as well. This would be the beginning of my love for skating, but that's another story.

There were the few kids I was aware of who had the newer, more expensive clothes or sneakers and shoes from retail stores, but still, there was something magical in these hand-me-downs. We were not self conscious about the lack of money or where we were on the food chain, because we were all in it together. It seemed like none of us were too worried about how we looked, or the status our clothes conveyed with brand names, if we were clean and presentable and had food in our bellies, nothing else really mattered?

Not to say I didn't have my favorite piece of clothing, that jean jacket which I had personalized by sewing on of the Canadian Fitness Award badges we use to get at school when we completed the different levels of the fitness program. Yes, everyone would make that clothing their own and take time to personalize it. Going to St. Agnes the first day after getting the hand-me-downs, everyone knew who was who in the zoo and you could see kids with a quizzical look in their eyes, as if they'd seen that shirt or jacket you had on with the stitching on the sleeve. It was like an open secret not spoken about, we just wore these clothes and got over it. There were occasions where someone would let it slip that that pair of pants you had on had been theirs at one time, and for a moment you would feel like a have-not, but that moment would pass very quickly, and what was said would be forgiven and forgotten.

I think that today we use clothes as a status symbol, a way to elevate ourselves. However, when I worked with kids in Ethiopia, Somalia, and Rwanda during my time in the military, and had friends send clothes over to me and gave my own away to them at the end of my tours, I soon realized the liberating power in those clothes for people in these countries. In many of these poorer places, I had the privilege to see that when you give hand-me-downs away, you give those in need, hope for their future and knowledge that there are others in the world who are concerned and connected enough to reach out to them. Giving hand-me-downs to another is never a problem. It is a small measure of kindness and hope to take the pressure off someone in need.

I am quite sure that my wearing hand-me-downs had served many purposes, both good and bad. Having been given these clothes at times, locked in my feelings of inadequacy and of knowing we may not have had as much as others, helped my coming to understand the social structure I was born into. As I grew into my teenage years back then, these differences became more apparent, because those who could afford the designer clothes or sneakers became the cool kids, and suddenly, after grade school, clothes became a status symbol and a way of differentiating yourself, exerting your economic standing in a peer group, and for some, letting those who couldn't afford newer clothes know their place on the food chain. This doesn't mean hand-me-downs as in and of themselves bad, the badness comes with the insecurities and class separation clothes can convey.

As I grow older, I have come to realize that I had to separate those things of childhood, which were blurred by time and the distance of a life that was. When I look back at my classmates from St. Agnes and later BEC, I know I wasn't the only one who grew up wearing a shirt too big or pants needing to be hemmed. For too long as an adult, I was burdened with the guilt of childhood and the belief that wearing hand-me-downs in some way made me a second-class citizen. But now, as I enter my later years, I look back with fondness and a better understanding of the love and compassion that was involved in a neighbourhood where everyone had a hand in me growing into who I am.

HOCKEY CARDS

'M NOT SURE WHEN I FELL IN LOVE WITH HOCKEY CARDS, BUT I THINK my first heroes, Bobby Orr and Derek Sanderson, had a lot to do with it. I used to go up to Buddy Graham's corner store, between MacDonald's Hardware and Woolworth's, to buy my cards all my years as a young kid. I would run up to the store as soon as the cards would come out, usually in early September. I would walk into Graham's store, and the sweet smell of the penny candy would hit me and my nostrils would flare out and take in the sweetness of those treats. My eyes would be as large as tea saucers as I looked through the counter window at all the penny candies it contained.

For ten or fifteen cents, you could get a whole bag full of penny candies, and I'm sure we would drive Emma, the lady waiting on us, crazy. We said, "I'll take two of those spearmint leaves, two honeymoon candies, three mojos, no, make that four. "It would take forever to pick a ten-cent bag of candy. Then, on the counter, would a box of hockey cards, glowing in their waxed paper packages with a shiny finish. You could feel the wax on your fingertips when you picked them up. They were twenty-five cents a pack, and usually had about eight cards, and a flat stick of bubble gum in them. I would get two packs at a time on most visits. After paying for the candy and cards, I would run home, sit on the veranda, and take joyful pleasure as I ate my candies while opening the fresh packages of hockey cards. I would line up, in my mind, the order of how the candies were to be eaten. First the spearmint leaves, then the chocolate covered honeymoons, and finally the mojos. I ate them last, because they were like toffee, and lasted the longest and had the sweetest taste.

While I was eating my candy, I would open the first pack of cards and smell them, that sweet flat stick of bubble gum with the white sugar powder, it would be overpowering in its aroma. When I had eaten all the candies, I'd fold this stick of gum in half and slowly chew it as my mouth filled up with its sweet flavour. Now, time to separate the hockey cards: first by the team, then by forwards, defence, and goalies. Then, I would have to look at the checklist, and check them off, so I knew what ones I had, and what doubles I had. This was all important information to an eight-year-old, because later, when you met up with the other boys in the neighbourhood, the trading would begin.

We knew that some of the cards were harder to get than the others, so these ones, we would hold for a premium when trading, and if you got a double one, it was like pure gold. I remember the boys from all over the neighbourhood would meet on the street to trade cards, some were older than myself. We would all meet with big fistfuls of hockey cards and I quickly caught on that some of the other boys would have tricks to try and steal cards from some of us smaller kids. One of their tricks would be shuffling cards from one hand to the other, thumb pushing them one by one form one hand to the other, and when they saw a card they liked, they would put their hand under their cap, as if they were scratching their head, and deposit the card they wanted under their baseball hat. I caught one of the boys doing this to me one time and grabbed my cards and ran home.

For the most part, we would just trade back and forth. When it was a premium card, one of our doubles, we could trade it for many lesser known players cards. I remember trading a double of Bobby Orr for five other cards. A pretty sweet deal, to a kid. Like the rest of the boys in the neighbourhood, I wanted to impress the others with my knowledge, of where the players were born, when they were drafted, what awards they had won, and their goals, assists, and penalty minutes. There would be the banter back and forth between us, all as we all tried to show how knowledgeable we all were. Some of the guys had quite the ability to recall the smallest of details and facts, which impressed everyone.

After spending a couple of hours out in the neighbourhood trading cards on Heelan Street, then going over to Second Street and doing the rounds with all the kids there, it would be time to go home and see how I did. I would lay out all the cards side by side, according to the teams. I would always sort out the original six first, then move onto the expansion teams, which were added in 1968, the Los Angeles Kings, Minnesota North Stars, California Seals, Philadelphia Flyers, Pittsburgh Penguins, and St. Louis Blues. I always was competitive with myself and tried to get the teams completed. I would trade within my house as well, with my older brother Kim. He was always harder to deal with than the boys in the street, but we usually worked it out, although I think looking back, he regularly did much better than I.

As I went from St. Agnes Elementary to BEC High School in 1976, I thought it was time to move on to new and better things. So, I put the cards in a shoebox and stored them in my closet. Years later, my little brother Kevin would find them, and play with them, and eventually most made their way to the garbage. But that was ok as I thought what are they for, if not to play with, look at, and enjoy?

When I joined the army and moved to Petawawa, I had Mom to pack up my remaining clothes and stuff from my bedroom at home and send it to me. It arrived a couple of weeks later, and there it was, a small box of hockey cards mostly from the mid seventies, and in relatively good shape. Sad thing was, when I first joined the military, I was only a private making a few hundred dollars a week and having a difficult time. So, one day, I took my cards to a local card dealer and when he saw them his face lite up, he knew they were valuable and although I knew I was getting a bad deal, sometimes when you are hungry, eating is more important than having cards you can only look at. So, I sold them for a couple hundred dollars. I often wonder what they would be worth in today's market.

I am glad that I had the experiences of collecting card then and not now. Today, I think much of the fun collecting hockey cards is gone. I watch the kids of today and the joy if collecting cards has been hijacked by adults, it's all about money and when you find a card of, say, Sidney Crosby, kids aren't allowed to play with it or touch it; it's put into a plastic case, sealed up, and then given a value. But the adults of today have forgotten the value of the card is in its being loved, being touched, perhaps stuck in your bicycle spokes, or shared amongst kids, not worshipped in plastic.

HOW DO YOU STOP A BULLY?

WAS IN GRADE NINE AT BRETON EDUCATION CENTRE AND AS I WAS leaving class one day, my math teacher stopped me, and said, "Lean against the door and look down the hallway, Derrick. Just keep looking down the hallway, don't say anything and listen to what I am going to say. See that big guy by the locker down there?" I looked down the hallway and this guy was standing there putting his books into a locker. I could see that he was a lot bigger than me with the size of a football fullback, probably around 180 pounds and 6 feet tall. Everyone in school knew who he was and his reputation as a bully! His picture could have been used in a dictionary next to the definition of bully, he truly was that guy everyone wanted to avoid. My teacher said, "Derrick, he's been picking on a much smaller guy for a while now. Do you think you could talk to him after school? "I said "Sure, Sir. Will do as soon as classes are over."

The smaller guy being picked on was only about 5'5" or so and his name was Allen. Although I never hung out with him, I knew he was a good young man, who just wanted to be left alone and attend school with as little turbulence as possible. His life had been a living hell for many years with this guy bullying him from his days in elementary school and now carrying on into high school. Every day, he would be harassed, punched, bumped into, hit, and teased.

After school, I caught up to the bully, and said, "Hey pal, can I talk to you for a minute?"

Looking at me and in a gruff voice he said, "What you want?" I said to him "Well, I hear that you've been picking on a guy half your size, and I think we need to talk about this."

He asked me what business was it of mine. I told him that I was making it my business, and he should try picking in someone his own size, like me. He said a few expletives towards me and then after a few minutes of staring me down, he jumped at me. We then began fighting and in the end after the fight was over, he understood I meant what I had said about picking on Allen. I told him that every time he picks on this kid, or anyone else for that matter and I hear of it, I wouldn't be too far behind and we would fight every time I saw him or heard of him bullying. Then, that was the end of it. I never mentioned it to anyone, nor spoke of it, and this guy never bothered the little or anyone else in school again after we had our little talk. What happened to the bully? Well, by grade ten, the he quit school and moved on.

Fast forward to the future after many years had passed. I had joined the army and gone to Somalia, Rwanda, and Bosnia and some 20 years had passed. Suddenly one day, while living in CFB Petawawa, Ontario, I get a letter in the mail and I didn't recognize the address or name. I opened it up and begin to read it.

It read:

Hi Derrick,

You probably don't remember me, but I was in the same grade as you, and although you never hung out with me, or even knew me, I was in the same grade with you through high school. I want to tell you that, up until grade nine, my life was miserable. Then, as the year was ending and I was going into grade ten, things began to change, and the bullying stopped, and life got better. I just thought it was that everyone was maturing going into senior high, but I found out that you had been my guardian, keeping watch over me, and I never knew that you had spoken to the guy who was bullying me. I just wanted to thank you for changing my life. It has meant a lot to me n my life, thanks.

I thought about it and remembered that day, that teacher, that bully, that little guy, and it all came back to me, and as I thought about it, I felt it was right thing to do back then, as it would still be today. It was good that I had a positive impact on another person's life. There are times when we are compelled to do what is right, and when we don't, we are just as wrong by watching. Raise your children to not be bystanders in life, but to stand up for what is right and help anyone who is down and needs that hand up.

I still have that letter and read it every so often to remind myself of what path I chose to take in life and what impact it had on that fellow all those years ago. I sometimes wonder of the others who were being bullied and I had done this for as well, hoping their lives were somewhat better for the efforts.

SHOVELLING THE NEIGHBOURHOOD OUT

As January began, the first major snowfall in the Winter 1973 wasn't far behind. School was cancelled for the day and we were all out playing and throwing snowballs. It was one of those winter days when it's cold, but there's enough moisture in the air to make the best snowballs and snowmen ever with your mittens and toque getting soaked in no time. I was only eleven at the time, and my brother thirteen. There were a few others from the neighbourhood with us, outside horsing around, throwing snowballs and wrestling in the snow, when someone came up with the idea to pool together all our labour, go around the neighbourhood to see if we could make some money shovelling snow for the day. It was decided that one of the older guys would be the front man, going up and establishing the "shovelling contract" and taking the money at the end of the day, to be split five ways amongst us.

With the amount of snow that fell, there was lots to shovel but we were eager to get at it. When I grew up, our entertainment was being outdoors, playing sports, kids games, and working when our parents needed something done and told us to get to it! Everyone had some type of physical chore as a child, so hard work was familiar to us, especially in those days of hauling out coal ashes, bringing in the coal buckets, and cutting the kindling. Before we had even begun to play that day, each of us had shovelled the driveways and walkways of our own houses.

The shovel I most liked to use was dad's big, coal miner's pan shovel. You could get a good pile of snow on this. It was probably half my size and it weighed a lot. During this time, there wasn't any Kevlar handles or lightweight metals such as aluminum. It was a good, old-fashioned hardwood shaft and metal blade that weighed as much as we did. I still remember how cold our hands got as we worked away, getting our gloves, toques and scarves wet with sweat. Once this happened, we would head to our home, or one of the other guy's homes, to get warmed up and then back to work quickly to continue with shovelling. If we went to our home, mom would make some tea for us, and there was always a nice piece of bread with butter on it. On occasion, my hands would be so cold, I could feel the stinging and prickles as they warmed up and began to thaw out. Mom would turn on the cold water and tell me to put my hands under the cold running water which would warm them up. I still do these things today after shovelling my driveway.

Once the tea was gone and warmed up, we headed back out and began shovelling all around the neighbourhood. We would be at it well into the early evening, never stopping, and by the end of the day we were cold, wet, and tired. I have my own children now, and it is seemingly impossible to get them out of the house, off their computers, to help me shovel the driveway. I think back to my time at their age, and think of the physical work we did. Not one of us complained, and most times weren't even told to go do it. We did it because we saw an opportunity for a few dollars, a few laughs and had fun along the way as we worked. I can't imagine telling my father, "No, I'm not going to shovel the driveway." We can talk about what would happen to me had I ever said that, but that's another story for another time.

I also think this childhood of physical work had set me up for continued success throughout my entire career in the military and in life, when times were tough or food was sparse, while deployed overseas and we hadn't fresh food or an abundance of water, I had already had similar experiences as a child. My baseline tolerance level was already set up from those earlier experiences. I had something which was difficult earlier in my life to contrast with and this made overseas tours easier for me.

As was the case with the older boys mentoring us younger kids in sports, so to was mentoring occurring here while shovelling. We were different ages, but I never recall any of the older boys complaining if one of us younger and smaller guys couldn't work as hard or shovel as much. We all still got the same amount of money at the end of the day. It was only a few dollars, but it was more than enough to go to the Paramount theatre and see *Snowball Express*, a Disney movie that was playing that weekend, with a bottle of double cola and some popcorn. That was it, and we were all content with the results of our hard day at snow shovelling.

LESSONS LEARNED FROM MY COACH

NEVER REALLY PLAYED ORGANIZED SPORTS UNTIL MY FIRST YEAR OF high school at Breton Education Centre in grade seven. I guess I was about twelve years old, and someone had mentioned to me about trying out for the soccer team, so I thought, why not? When tryouts arrived, I showed up that day with my t-shirt and shorts, then suddenly I realized that this was the senior boys' team, and got to wondering, "what am I doing here?" Regardless, I was here now having showed up, and was determined to do my best.

The beginning was easy, a warm up, some running but then it got a little more difficult, when the coach started talking what seemed a foreign language. He was speaking about a "floating off side" and going "shoulder to shoulder" with an opponent and something about a "calling for a ball." I was baffled for a little while until I learned the soccer terms, but it quickly came. The rest of the guys were already comfortable with this as most had been playing for years and this my first attempt. I was fortunate that I had a little skill, was adaptable and in pretty good shape so could keep up, which seemed to be what the coach favored the most.

The coach for the boys' team was Mr. Terry MacSween, and I guess the first thing he taught me was not to take things personally. He would to say to us, "There are two rules in life. The first is don't sweat the small stuff, and the second is that everything is small." I guess, not having ever played before in organized sports, I was making lots of mistakes and errors and really didn't now the rules. But Terry was there to encourage me, as were the older guys on the team. If during a game, I missed a kick, and the ball passed by me, it was never critical. There was an "Ok,

Derrick, let's get over that and get our head into the game," but always in a supportive manner. I took this lesson from life and used it all during my career in the military. While deployed overseas, there were times of immense pressure, bad guys trying to hurt you, injured troops you are trying to care for or save, but I always remembered, "Don't sweat the small stuff, and everything is small." You need to put it all in perspective. We are all in this together, so support one another, don't knock each other down.

The thing Terry was strict on was attending practice. We practiced some mornings and every day after school. The junior guys would get together on the weekend and practice, practice, and practice. I knew I could never be a Pele, but I could be the best Derrick if I kept practicing those areas which needed improvement in my game, this was another lesson I took from soccer. When I went to Afghanistan and we were training, we had some incredible leaders, just as we had had incredible soccer players as leaders in high school. We can achieve whatever we challenge ourselves to achieve, we just need to work hard, and not to be tied down with false comparisons and judging yourself by another's measuring stick. I was never the best soldier, but as a soldier I always tried my best. Terry used to tell us to see the ball in front of you, but to have your peripheral vision always scanning, focus on what you can control, not what the other guy is doing. Far too often today, people watch others, compare themselves to others, and talk about others. Terry taught me to control myself, my emotions, and my actions, as that's all I can really control. I can't control that player in front of me or the heckler on the sideline.

This lesson came back to me one day while deployed. I remember one terrible day in Afghanistan, there was intense fighting going on close by and I had a truck with eleven Afghani soldiers brought to my aid station. I was overwhelmed for a fleeting moment, but I slowed it down, looked at what I had in front of me, and enlisted the help of other non-medical people around me. At that point in time, working together as a team to save these men's lives was all that mattered. It was our main objective to get these guys home to their wives and children, get them home alive. And to do so I looked to my front, focused on what I could control, no matter what chaos was going on around me.

I used to go downtown at night with my soccer ball up until grade ten, juggling it, kicking it off the wall in front of the post office. My thirst for knowledge of the game was there all the years I played, until at forty years old had knee surgery. But when I could, I kept playing and trying different moves which allowed me to always improve and be the best that I could be. It's important to learn and to be open to change. The one constant in life is change, if you cannot accept this, it will be a hard life for you. I took this lesson and it served me extremely well in life and at work. We were always learning new medical procedures, techniques, and protocol changes, and if I hadn't stayed open and accepting of this, then I couldn't have continued as a Physician assistant. I was always involved, and still am, in lifelong learning. No matter what we think, we don't know it all, and learning daily helps us to develop and stay active.

I think one of the most important lessons I learned from Terry, and it would serve many young people today, is attitude. An attitude can be a good or bad one, and it's up to the individual. If something goes wrong, and instead of addressing it right there, you stew on it and develop a bad attitude, it affects everyone. There was one time I was in my last year of playing high school soccer and figured that making the team would be a no brainer. After the last day of tryouts for the soccer team, the list would be posted the next day on bulletin board by the main office. I ran down after last class of the morning to check and looked up and down the list for my name, but saw that my name never made the list. I was hurt, angry and sad. I went home and my mother asked me if I made the team again, and I said no. I told her that I had checked the list down on the bulletin board and my name wasn't there. Boy, my attitude took a drastic change for the worse and I was miserable. A few days later, I got a call from Terry. He said, "Derrick, I hear you think you didn't make the team. It was an honest mistake, and I forgot to put your name on. So, get over it grizzle head and get to practice right now!" At that moment, I learned that, sometimes things may go wrong, and the only thing you really control is the way you react to it. Looking back, whether I made the team or not shouldn't have been that negative.

We were once playing against a new team in the high school league and we were winning by 4-0 at halftime, Terry spoke to us, and said, "Guys, remember when you were coming together as a team a few years back and you were losing more than winning. Now you are winning more than losing, but never forget where you came from and never run the score up on anyone that may not be as good as you. We were all new at one time so stay humble." We were taught that be a good winner as well as a good loser and never show off, so for the rest of the game we passed the ball and eased off the offense, we realized that there was no value in humiliating this new team. As was the tradition, at the end of the game we lined up and shook hands and told them they played well.

When my youngest child was five, we were playing in a recreation soccer league, it was the parents that were emphasizing winning or how many goals their children got. I had to go back into the memory bank of my life and find this lesson there and remind them that win, lose, or draw, this is supposed to be fun, and the way the parents act, and react, affects this for their children.

I think one of the most important lessons I learned from Terry was to be a team player. He would say, "Leave it all on the field." I really understood his words when I was deployed to Afghanistan in 2007, and we lost twelve soldiers in the infantry company I was attached to. It would be here I learned the real lesson of leaving it all on the field, about struggling to save my comrades, and not giving up. I learned to leave it all on the field, and after this tour, came back home with little left in the tank. To many, it's only a soccer game, but for my thirty-five years in the military, Terry's words often served as a benchmark for me to be a better human, a better soldier, and to never quit, no matter what the odds or obstacles.

LIVING ROOM
OUT OF BOUNDS

A S A SMALL CHILD, I WAS OUT PLAYING ONE BEAUTIFUL WARM summers day and on returning home in the afternoon, I walked into the house and saw the living room filled with brand new furniture. Unbeknownst to me, mom and dad had been speaking with Mr. Al Bernick and had ordered the new chesterfield and chair. Al Bernick was the furniture guy in New Waterford everyone went to, and he had payment plans for those who needed to purchase new furniture. He was a humble man, serving many of the coal miners families of New Waterford, and for many, payment plans would be the only way they could afford to purchase new furniture and appliances. He would bring the furniture and then every Thursday, which was the coal mines payday, we would see him driving all over town, dropping by the coal miners' homes collecting five or ten dollars, whatever the family could afford that week. There was never pressure, just what the family could afford until it was paid.

There were also times when a family member of the community passed away and the family couldn't afford a suit for the funeral. Mr. Bernick would quietly stop by the family's home and offer to provide a suit for free. This was only but one of the ways he gave back to his community, something many would never find out until years later, as he was a modest man who avoided public accolades for these acts of kindness.

Looking in at the new furniture in the living room, all glowing in its newness, I could smell the freshness of the material, and it was all fully wrapped with plastic slipcovers. Yes, plastic! It was all the rage at the time and I happened to witness this plastic trend as part of my youth. It was like the furniture was in protective custody, but from who or what I never knew? However, looking back now, that was easy to answer. It was us kids, as every house during this time had five or more kids. I remember the families around New Waterford with five, ten, or more kids, and the peanut butter and jam sandwiches, muddy sneakers, and open-faced glasses with fruit juice, all of which when dropped, spilt, or kicked onto the couch would somehow make it melt, sort of like the evil witch on *The Wizard of Oz*.

Plastic slipcovers were there to signify that this was a special place, held in high esteem, and usually only visited by adults. The plastic slipcovers acted somewhat as a visible barrier, sort of like those rope barriers you would see at museums or theatres. All you needed was a red carpet into the porch and a doorman to complete the scene. As a child, we felt it was probably a cool place to go and see, to investigate what was behind that rope, but us kids couldn't get in, as we were too young and the front room was for the adults only. When I think back, I laugh at those plastic covers and what they represented. Was it trying to better ourselves, or maybe the fact that new furniture wasn't common, so best take care of it. Whatever it was all about is still up for debate all these years later.

I wondered why our chesterfield and living room furniture was so protected, like an endangered species down to its last breeding pair? The living room was a place not for us dirty, greasy, little kids. No, it was reserved for "guests," when mom's friends would drop by, and of course, she would make a sandwich and tea for them, as they sat there in that land of plastic slipcovers we wanted to ascend to some day. But, this was the time, as my dad use to tell me, that "kids should be seen and not heard" and "only speak when your spoken to." These ideas now are viewed as being very strange and antiquated, but perhaps they served the purpose of making us wait, making us listen, and not be the center of attention.

Looking back now, it certainly wasn't the kids who had the run of the house, no, we were confined to the TV room and kitchen for the most part. Everything else was reserved for adults or special holiday meals. The front room (living room), and dining room were non-starters.

I remember giggling with my brother and sister, as we would sit on the heavy grade vinyl chesterfield cover, and almost immediately hear the squeaking, crinkling of the vinyl, and it sticking to our bare legs as we sat there in our shorts in the hot and humid summer day. Getting up from the chesterfield, you could feel your sticky skin slowly lifting off the vinyl slipcover, and then as you touched your legs, you could feel all the sweat on them from sitting too long in one place.

I often wondered about this phenomenon of plastic slipcovers. Was it just a part of the new-found growth of consumerism and parents who were made feel this was needed, or if it was that most moms and dads back then were suffering from OCD (Obsessive Covering Disease)? Was it just the fact that they grew up in the shadow of the worst war mankind had ever seen? Most of our parents were brought up during difficult times and had to make do with what they had. There was a frugality within all of them, which many of us boomers never really understood. During our parents' childhoods, food was rationed, money was extremely hard to come by and working in the mines or raising a family even harder. For many, it was that once in a lifetime purchase, because with all us baby boomer children under foot, when would you have the chance to buy new again?

As time went by, and we passed from childhood to our teenage years, I saw the use of those vinyl slipcovers decline. I think it was because of the invention of new and improved upholstery materials, or perhaps it was that the teenagers of the sixties and seventies saw their homes as spaces to live in, and parents accepted the fact that to live in a space, it will get dirty and untidy, that babies and kids like to touch. Maybe it was the introduction of those low-cost furniture stores and mass production which made chesterfields and modern furniture cheaper.

Back then, the living room space was for the adults and was theirs alone, and although I certainly didn't understand it then, as the years have passed I do understand that our moms and dads worked hard for everything they got. All the parents in New Waterford took very little for themselves, and it was always what was best for the family that was utmost to them. So, what was the harm in being proud of your furniture, protecting it and admiring it? We might all do well to look back and emulate these days gone by.

MENTORING—
THE VALUE OF
GROWING UP IN
NEW WATERFORD

REMEMBER WHEN I WAS A LITTLE BOY, I ALWAYS WANTED TO HANG around my big brother, Kim. It must have been a pain in the arse for him. Everywhere he went, I would follow, like a lost puppy. I remember some of his friends found me a bother as well, because I was always pushed to the back, or roughed up, not in a bad way, more like play fighting. But I was kept close enough so I wouldn't get lost. All the kids in the neighbourhood would find their ways to Second Street, where there was an old ball field. It was just an open field on the other side of the brook, across from No. 12 Colliery.

There would be a large group of us kids who would spontaneously show up every afternoon during the summer. There wasn't one adult around to be found, just the older kids, who usually had their younger brothers and sisters with them. The two oldest boys would run the show. First, they would throw a bat in the air and grab it, then work their way to the top, hand over hand. The one who covered the top of the bat got to pick first.

Then they would tell us to line up in a single file, all twenty or so of us. Then, the two older boys would take a pick each, back and forth, back, and forth. "I'll take Johnny." "I'll take Bob." "Let me have Tommy." "Okay. I'll take Dave." I was always one of the last to be picked, but in later years to follow, would eventually move up the line, taking my place and becoming one of the older boys who ran the show and mentoring the younger kids. After the teams were picked, it seemed that almost always both teams were well balanced, so from the start, we knew that either team could win, and every play mattered, even if it was just about playing and having fun.

So here we were, a bunch of unsupervised kids, between seven and fifteen. We all took to the game what we had, some old gloves, bats, a couple of sweaters for the bases, and lots and lots of kids from all over the neighbourhood. Occasionally, we would hear a mother's scream. "DAAAAAVVIIIIID, GET HOME, NOW!" However, this never affected the game, because we were like rabbits, you take two of us away, then another four would show up, the game went on for hours.

The game was based on the honour system. Even the opposite team would say, "No, that was a strike," even when it was against their own team, there were never adults around to impose rules; it was kids leading kids. We just all played, and everything usually went smoothly. For sure, occasionally there would be conflicts, or a moment when someone threatened to go home if they didn't get their way, which might have been the end of the game. This is where the mentorship of the older boys would kick in. They would ask, "What's wrong Billy?" Then Billy would begin, "I wanted to play shortstop, but got put in the outfield, and no one's hitting to me. I'm going to take my baseball bat and go home." It was at this moment everyone would realize that Billy had the only bat, and if he went home, the game was over! So, the older boys would smooth things over and ask Dave if he could go outfield for a while and let Billy play shortstop. It would all work out and the game continue, but we all learned a little during these times of negotiation and calming the waters, useful tools for later in life.

The best was the pure fun and honesty of the games. No one cheated or lied. If it was a strike, everyone would call out "strike," and we all knew it was. Same with a fly ball; if it was on the line, or even close, it would be called foul. This is just how it was. It wasn't about being overly competitive. It was about being outside, on a field, with a group of friends, having fun.

It was so innocent during these times, growing up in New Waterford. I always liked watching Carl Yastrzemski from the Boston Red Socks, so I would imagine that I was him when I played. There was no pressure, and if you struck out, the rest would say, "Hey Derrick, great try maybe next time." We would play for hours, lose count of the score, then remember the last score we could think of and go from there. No problem and no fighting, it just was what it was, and we were all having fun.

At eight thirty, the air raid siren would scream across town, telling kids under sixteen to get home. We knew it was ending for the night, so the one of the older boys would say, "Next run wins!" No one cared who won, and no one ever remembered. A ball would be "smashed" to the outfield, and a run scored just in time, when suddenly we would hear a symphony of moms screaming their kid's names. "Bobby, get home now!" and "Derrick, Kim, get in the yard before I send your father!" By the time the curfew whistle quieted, we would we would all be home to our yards, back to home base, safe at the end of the day.

I now live in Pembroke, Ontario across from a lighted ball field. Seldom do I see a pick-up game in the neighbourhood, or even unaccompanied kids running around. The way we played in the sixties and seventies, from pick-up baseball to pick-up road hockey, kick the can at night, these simple games and unsupervised time taught all of us to develop independence, negotiating, and problem-solving skills. The older boys taught us to organize, set goals and rules, to have a sense of honesty and respect for one another. We all inherently knew that this was the right and fair way to be. No one had to tell us. It had been mentored this way for years and years, and I was fortunate enough to carry this forward into the eighties as I was finishing high school.

When I look back, it's with fondness at these spontaneous, pick-up games, which were there to teach us. It was competitive, but we were not sticklers on rules. It was a time for everyone to be treated fairly, whether you were a good athlete or not. It was exciting to be part of a team and be with those you looked up to. No one ever got hurt, and it was the neighbourhood that raised a child; we raised each other during these times, in many respects.

Later in life, I coached soccer for a few years with my own kids, and I think there are many lessons from my youth in New Waterford that would serve many of today's parents and children well, lessons of having fun, keeping it simple and fun for all kids, keeping things competitive enough to make it interesting, but friendly enough for everyone to know they had contributed.

There are times when I go through my box of goodies from growing up as a kid, while everyone is still sleeping, and let my mind wander back to that place back then, my childhood. Occasionally, I will pull out on my old baseball glove and look at my hand in it. I will make a fist with my other hand and hit the pocket of the glove and for a moment, be back there on the field with the others playing a pick-up game.

MINERS'
SUMMER VACATION

EVERY SUMMER, WE WOULD ANTICIPATE THE END OF JULY. THIS was when all the coal miners would look forward to their two weeks' vacation, the last week of July into the first week of August. As kids, we were filled excitement, as we knew it was during this time when dad would have his yearly break and be home with us for awhile. Of course, there would be the things to do around the home, windows, and roof to be fixed, fences to be mended, and maybe even some vacationing away from Cape Breton Island.

This was the time our fathers took home their work clothes and the thick, warm jackets worn in the deep of the coal mines. The miners would take them home for cleaning during vacation time, and within a day or two of vacation's beginning, their work clothes would be scrubbed, washed, and then hung out on clothes lines across New Waterford, a sort of flag of freedom from the cold belly of the coal mine. Unless you were born into this time and place, I believe it may be difficult to fully understand how hard these men worked in those terrible conditions, and how much they looked forward to this short reprieve. The long, forty-minute trips down the main deep to the coal face, the breathing in of thick coal dust, which would eventually steal their ability to breath, the cold and dampness of the mines. All of this was difficult for even families of what the miners were living through, to fully appreciate and understand at the time.

I cannot imagine in my own life having only two weeks off in the summer and a few extra days' vacation at Christmas, cannot imagine working in the darkness of the earth for forty-nine weeks a year.

Growing up in my neighbourhood there was never a shortage of widows, a seemingly bumper crop, but for us to see older men around town was extremely rare.

During this two-week vacation, some miners would take their families on trips, but many couldn't afford these vacation trips, so instead would go camping on Sangaree Island, which was owned by St. Agnes Church. After spending forty-nine weeks in a dark and cold mine with air from the surface being pumped underground and mixed with the methane gas and coal dust in the air, there was no greater desire for these fathers and husbands than to get away from the darkness and deep of the mine, to be out in open spaces, where the air was clean, where the sun was bright and family present.

Not all miners went on trips or camping during their vacations, though. Some, such as my dad, just wanted to be around the house and left to their own devices. I don't ever remember our family going on a trip or taking a vacation, and I don't believe we were the exception. I think it was commonplace to stay at home during this time, as money was usually tight, and trips were an unnecessary waste of money. Money which could go into other, more important things, with winter around the corner. My dad would just tinker around fixing things around the house for the upcoming winter. Of course, the annual Circus would come to town, and that would be the major excitement for the first week of their vacation, this was also a time for the entire family to do something together.

The anticipation for the circus began when posters started popping up in stores around town, stapled to light posts. It was advertised for weeks prior to their arrival. You could feel the entire town was excited. Then, a day or two before it was to begin, there would be a truck convoy straight down Plummer Avenue, with the rides and sleeping trailers on them, seemingly parading down the street as they announced their arrival. I remember myself, and other kids around the neighbourhood, running down on that first day to watch them setting up. They always set up on the ball field on the corner of Plummer and 13th Street.

As we all tried to look behind the baseball field fence what was going on, all we could see were the silhouettes of the men's figures behind the burlap that hung around the baseball field fence, encompassing the circus as they worked. Slowly, you would see, rising over the fence, some of the rides as they were being put together and constructed. The Ferris wheel would be one of the first peeking over and all us kids were along the fence getting more excited, watching as other rides began rising.

Finally, once the rides and tents were all out together, the circus would open the next day. My older brother Kim and I, along with our little sister Andrea, would have to wait until later that first evening, when Mom would take us down. She loved to go every year and play the circus bingo, where instead of money they would give circus credits. Mom would play around sixteen cards, and at the top of all the tables were these gutters filled up with kernels of corn used for marking the cards. When someone would get a bingo, they would get wooden coupons with number value stamped on them. After Mom was done playing, she would go to the long table at the front of the tent where all the prizes were held, exchanging these coupons for household items. I remember one year her picking out a nice pair of table lamps, taking them home, she was so proud of her winnings on this occasion. Mom always enjoyed circus bingo and knowing she enjoyed this, we would encourage her to keep playing, because we knew if she was sitting there playing bingo, we would still be there at the circus having fun!

While Mom was doing this, I went buzzing around with all the lights, sounds, and sweet smells of cotton candy, popcorn, and candy apples. I still can feel a warm, summer's-night's soft breeze and the excitement the circus brought to town. Unlike now, when you can buy cotton candy anytime, this was our only time of the year to get the delicious, fluffy treat. I remember the smells of the cotton candy and popcorn wafting throughout the entire area.

The excitement of the rides was not just in the ride itself, but when I would be in motion and the coloured lights and people walking by were a blur and the thrill of feeling butterflies in the pit of your stomach as the ride whipped around. The loud, tinny circus music filled the air and invited us to the different rides throughout the grounds, mixed with the barkers calling out from the games set up in long rows between the rides.

There were people everywhere. It seemed as thought the whole town had come on this opening night. The operators of the rides were rough looking men, usually with lots of tattoos, which in those days were seldom seen, and always barking out as you walked by the games they operated, trying to get you to use your tickets on a ride or play one of the games, which no one ever seemed to win.

The games were never easy to win. Those running the games made it look easy, as they would knock down all the milk bottles with one mighty throw of a baseball. But no one else could repeat this feat. The prizes were usually cheap stuffed animals and toys, but this being a small town, they seemed somehow exotic, and all the girls wanted their boyfriends to win one of the big, stuffed animals for them. In earnest, the boyfriend would spend all his money, trying to use his might to knock down the milk bottle, in a jocular attempt at impressing his girl and winning her the big teddy bear, while being slowly drained of all his money. With young love being what it was, they were easy picking for these seasoned carnival games operators.

Unlike today, when you can fly a remote helicopter and get an aerial view on New Waterford, back then, my only hope to get above the trees and buildings to see town was through riding on the Ferris wheel. When it reached the highest point, as they were loading riders on below, you would have a few moments when it was still, to scan the town and all its landmarks. You could look all the way up to the New Waterford Consolidated Hospital and to its left see Mount Carmel Church. Or you could look straight down Plummer Avenue and see all the cars cruising the main drag and the young couples waiting in line outside the Paramount theatre. If you stretched and strained your eyes hard enough, you could see the steeple of St. Agnes Church and the No. 12 Colliery Bankhead on the horizon. As the wheel began going around, once it was full of passengers, I liked to sit back in my seat and look up at the sky and stars as we spun around and watched them passing. With the flashing lights, the games, and all the town in attendance, this yearly event is easily one of my fondest memories growing up in New Waterford.

The last week of vacation, dad like to go out to Laffin's Cove or over to Dominion Beach where we would swim for hours, afterwards going over to the sandbar side to dig for a feed of clams to take home. While we were doing these things, he would just sit on the beach and watch the ocean. Maybe it was just his time to recharge, after all, being ten miles under the Atlantic Ocean with the risk of a mine cave in always on your mind, it must do something to a person.

Dad would take a daily pilgrimage up to his favourite place, Dave Wilkie's Barber Shop. Most other miners would go to one of the local barber shops around town as well, to talk hockey, baseball, and of course, the coal mine. Others would take a break and have a beer at the local Belmont Tavern or one of the other taverns in town, where all the men would gather and continue their talk about hockey, sports, and of course, coal mining. Dad enjoyed sitting on our front veranda and watching everyone, as they walked by the house. Occasionally, Mel Quinn, or one of his other friends would stop by and sit for hours on the veranda and just talk, having a cigarette and coffee.

Miners' vacation was also a time for me to get to know dad a little more. During vacation, he would always be up early, when everyone was still in bed. He wasn't one to talk a lot to us as children. I would take out my little record player and put on some of his old records of Glenn Miller and Tommy Dorsey. I could see him revisiting in his mind those times of his youth when he was driving big cars, going to see the big bands of that time, and it would be during this time, as I played records, when he would speak about those times of his youth. He would tell me stories about growing up in the forties and fifties, of his brothers and sisters, the grandfather and grandmother whom I had never met, and of his childhood growing up in New Victoria.

As miners' vacation ended, the nights would become cooler as leaves began to change their colour, both a reminder that the first day of school was not far behind. The exciting events of the circus would remind all of us of summer's close and of fall's entrance, with the change of the leaves and explosion of colours that was to bring.

The day would come when miners' vacation was over. We would be reminded on a Sunday night of the end of miner's vacation as we came in from another summer's night of playing baseball or soccer with the neighbourhood kids. There it would be, on the kitchen countertop, the evidence that the time has come, dad's steel lunchbox and next to it his check number. In the fridge would be some sandwiches and a couple of bottles of water for that night, as he prepared to go in on backshift as vacation ended.

I still think back to those times and to the austerity of the work they did, knowing that their time had come and gone, and they were now working for our futures, personally sacrificing so much as parents to ensure that we had a way out, a way to a better life. This was the best of times for all of us back then, although we would only realize this with the passage of time.

ROTE LEARNING
AT ST. AGNES

REMEMBER BEING IN MY GRADE FOUR CLASS WITH MRS. OLIVER, A class of over thirty kids. Our generation was the tail end of the "Baby Boomer" and looking back, I think we were an interesting, and occasionally, rowdy bunch. This alone could have been the sole reason I respected my teachers, but no there was so much more that made me respect them, a firm hand and ability to take charge of us through all the highs and lows of our youth, uploading us with essential knowledge. However, as I grow older and listen to my own children's experiences in school, I reflect on the times growing up in the sixties. It was just the teacher and usually a yard stick to keep us in line, if this didn't work, well there was always the strap. For myself, the strap and I were on first name basis until my last year at St. Agnes, which ended after grade six.

I recall the way we were taught back then as well, mostly everything was by rote learning, whether that be math, science, spelling, even down to manners. I imagine it was thought back then, and they were mostly right, that by continual repetition we would eventually memorize what was essential, and through this, make the leap to being able to apply that knowledge. It was certainly a strict and disciplined approach, but seemingly it worked for most of us.

I remember from our very beginnings, we were taught that when another teacher, or adult, entered the classroom to stand up and greet them. We did this as a group, and it was drilled into us. In retrospect, I think this was a good thing to teach us, it instilled manners and respect for our elders and adults. Even today, I do this with my own children. I don't allow friends, when they come to my house, to give my kids "knuckles." That might be ok on a sports field, however at home we need to model the behaviour we want from our children. I was taught to shake hands, can you imagine going for a job interview and when your potential employer puts out his hand, you give him knuckles because that's what you were taught at home? No, this isn't right. We are the first examples our children see, then at school it is the teachers who have so much influence, and for us they carried out their duties meticulously.

Learning things by rote memory, or "learning by heart", happens naturally, when you think of it, when Mom or Dad would read over and over and over the story of Cinderella, or The Big Bad Wolf, or sing "Rock a Bye Baby." After a couple of times, we knew it, every single word. This was how we learned to sing, to read, to write, to be able to go to the store for our parents or neighbours. And when I knew I might get a nickel or a dime for running to Buddy Graham's Store, I could remember almost *anything*.

My childhood schooling was what they now call a "chalk and talk" education, with our teacher up front of the blackboard and us sitting at our old wooden desks. It was drilled into our brains, from that first day of school, that the three R's (Reading, Writing and 'Rithmatic) were the be all and end all of our days at school, and these subjects were going to be memorized by rote learning. When my daughter Hannah was in grade three and having difficulty with her times tables, I decided to go old school and did some rote learning with her. I would start with the one-times-tables, and over the weeks, worked up to the ten-times-tables. I would say each line. "Hannah, one times one equals one. Two times two equals two." with this she would repeat back to me, and on and on, until she had memorized them all.

Hannah asked me one day, "Daddy, why do we need to memorize the times tables?" I told her it's important and that when an opportunity presented I would show her. Then one day the opportunity arrived. We were shopping at the grocery store and the teller had made an error in the numbers, I always follow along while the order is being rung through and usually I am aware roughly, within a few cents, what the cost at the end will total. On this one day, when it was a little more like a few dollars over, I questioned the teller. When she looked at the list, she noticed there had been an error in entering the quantity. With this little error, my chance to show Hannah why it was important to memorize times tables presented. I told her, "See, if I couldn't multiply in my head and know how to round up or down, I would have assumed the computer was right and had paid almost ten dollars too much. This is one of the reasons why it's important to memorize."

As kids, we had to memorize poetry and recite it back, word for word, as well. If I just put a few lines to some poetry from that time here, "Whose woods these are I think I know. His house is in the village though." I would bet most reading this would remember these words as the beginnings of Robert Frost's "Stopping by Woods on a Snowy Evening." I can still recite this as well as "The Road Not Taken," and Leigh Hunt's "Abou Ben Adhem." We would have to go home after school and write these over ten times, reciting them aloud as we wrote. Along with this would be the requirement to have neat handwriting, which to my amazement is no longer taught in schools as the computer and tablets have replaced the need to do cursive writing. One lesson lead into the other throughout our educational development, building slowly, and once the foundation laid, on to other things, like studying nature and bringing things from our everyday experiences to school—a bee hive, a bird's nest, or a few pressed leaves and flowers in the fall, or a bag of tadpoles in the spring. We would take leaves and put them between wax paper, then put a cloth over the wax paper, and then iron them, eventually making a mobile for our parents.

Miss Carol Richardson was also a follower of rote learning, with us having to memorize all our songs. And if you were in the ukulele group, learning by rote how to read music. Then, there was that old, mid-century cloth map of Canada, and with her pointer, Mrs. Oliver would drill in the provinces, territories, and all the capitals into our memories. There was the reading in class, and everyone had to take their turns reading aloud, as the teacher walked up and down the aisles, stopping by each of us when it was our turn. Sometimes, there would be the fun of boys against the girls with a classroom spelling bee, when we lined up on either side of the classroom. Going back and forth spelling words of increasing difficulty, until there were only two remaining, then finally a winner.

I must admit that our old school teachers knew what they were doing. They were building a foundation that would last into our adulthood. They knew we needed to have the fundamentals before we could go off and begin connecting these concepts together. I was lucky to have teachers who taught me that information, without understanding, is just information, and that the important work we did was in us having an inquisitive and thoughtful mind, bringing that knowledge to a useful purpose.

I am sure that Mrs. Oliver and the rest of the teachers who came into my life at St. Agnes knew that everything they were teaching was laying down the foundation for the rest of my life. Later when I was teaching my own children the old-school method of doing the times tables, we all enjoyed that time together. While writing this, I had an epiphany and it was that I am so thankful to my teachers, because of their efforts in making me memorize. It means that I own this knowledge, it's mine and mine alone, and I will never have to google what twelve times twelve is, or a beautiful Robert Frost poem. Thanks to all my teachers for the investment in me. You have had a great impact on me becoming who I am, and I will be forever thankful.

WATCHING DAD SHAVE

AVE YOU EVER JUST TAKEN A MOMENT IN TIME AND FOCUS on a singular event that took place when you were a kid, really look at that one event and wonder what it was, or what it is, that brings you back to that moment in time? I very often do and find now entering into my late 50's, I do even more, but this is not a bad thing as it is important to have all these memories.

I remember as a little kid watching my dad as he prepared for work at 12 Colliery, I don't know why but watching him gave me a sense of security and the pride he took in preparing for work. The first thing he would do was to pack his lunch. Mom had made some sandwiches and wrapped a few cookies, so he would place it in his lunch can, then fill up his water bottle and putting it into the fridge until he was ready to leave, it was always the last thing to go into the lunch can before leaving. Then dad would go to the kitchen sink and prepare for a quick shave prior to heading to work.

Dad would take out his old Gillette double headed razor and Old Spice shaving cup, which had the bar of shaving soap in it with the foaming brush to apply it to his face. I also remember that "safety razor", it had a wide head on it and on the bottom of the handle was where he would have twisted it, to open the top up which contained the double-sided blade. On turning the handle, the two little metal doors would open exposing the razor blade which sat in a recess under the doors. Then dad would take out the old blade and insert a new one then close it. Usually a blade would last him for a week or so depending on how often he shaved.

I would place myself next to him there in the kitchen by the sink, from here I would watch him as he went about his shaving routine. As a child I was fascinated with the whole procedure as he would wash his face with hot water and bar soap to soften up the whiskers, then taking the foaming brush and adding hot water to the cup, he would then whip up the soap to a foamy lather then applied it to his face in small circles. I don't know why it was, but there was something about watching dad shave, the simple act of doing this seemed so hypnotizing and something which only dads did. When he was finished one again he looked like the dad I had always known.

He would go from a rough whiskered face, to a soft and smooth face, as I would watch he would take the shaving brush and rub a little of the foam on my face and laugh. After he finished shaving, sometimes there would be small nicks where he cut himself and he would take a pencil and touch the spots and they would magically stop. Following this would be the "Old Spice" after shave which we had bought him for Christmas or the aftershave mom had bought from the Avon lady who usually made her rounds all over town at the end of each month, and he had gotten for Fathers Day. Sometimes after dad went to work, I would go into the cupboard and take out his mug and soap dish and looking into the mirror do the exact steps my dad had done in preparation for shaving. I would pretend to shave off the foam using a popsicle stick as I was still afraid to try the real razor.

I remember during the winter of 1981 when dad had surgery, and into March or 1982 as he was getting sicker, it was during this last year of his life where dad continued to work in the mine, like an old pit horse until he could do so no more. In late February, they called an ambulance to Lingan Mine, he was in so much pain and couldn't bear it any longer, they took him directly to the New Waterford hospital, he had been diagnosed a year earlier with stomach cancer found on surgery. With little of the benefits we have today, he kept working to feed his family, even while he was in immense pain for that entire year leading to his passing. I think back to that the last day I visited him in the hospital, the last day he was alive. He had a dignity about him and with knowing the end was coming, he was extremely sad knowing that he would soon be leaving us but resigned to this fate. He told me that his friend, Dave Wilkie, had been there for a visit the night before and had brought his clippers, and had given him a haircut and shave, he was a proud man and there was a pride in how he wanted to present himself, even as he waited for death his grooming and how others saw him was important.

As I prepared to leave the hospital, not knowing it would be the last time I would see dad, I looked for a moment at him all clean and shiny, well groomed with a nice haircut and clean-shaven face, so soft and gentle. This was what matter to him to be always clean and presentable, in the end allowed him to have his dignity as he prepared to die. My last memory of dad was when I bent over him as he lay on the hospital bed and I hugged him and kissed his cheek one last time, feeling his soft skin on my cheek and that familiar smell of dad, with this last good-bye kiss, I left telling him, "see you later dad", not knowing that this was never to be as he passed away only a few hours later. I still have the memories of that last time I saw him and having been afforded the chance to say that one last "Goodbye".

Today, I still have my fathers Old Spice cup and brush as well as that old Gillett double head razor. Although I don't use it any longer for personal shaving it still holds lots of memories for me. When Dad passed away, for the first few years I used it and even took it on tour to Somalia with me, one of my first tours in the military. This razor and shaving cup represented the memories as to what a father should be, the bearings to be a man and follow him, to have integrity, be humble and work hard.

Now it is my son who watches me as I shave, and it is now I who am putting a little blob of shaving cream on his nose. As he giggles when wiping it away, thoughts of my dad are never far behind.

NEIGHBOURHOOD STORE RUNNER

When I was a growing up on Heelan Street, I had no grandparents living except my grandfather, who lived in Toronto who we never saw often. My father's parents had both passed away before my birth, my grandmother on mom's side had passed when mom was very young and she had no contact with my grandfather. By default, all the men and women of my neighbourhood became my surrogate grandparents, and they we as close to me as I imagine any grandparents would have been.

I remember being the runner for everyone in the neighbourhood. They would call Mom and say, "Hello, Patsy, is Derrick around to run up to Buddy Graham's?" and off I was. I ran to the store for years for Mrs. Stanford, Isabel Timmons, Agnes Bates, Fruity McKinnon, and so many others. This fell onto me because I was a couple of years younger than the rest of the boys in the neighbourhood, so when they were away at Sangaree Summer Camp, or hanging out, I was often left to my own devices. What I remember mostly was knocking on the doors of the person I was going to the store for, and when they opened, the smells of the cooking pouring out from their kitchens. It filled my nostrils with the smells of fresh baked bread, cookies, the smell of a roast, carrots, and potatoes. Scent memories like these flood back to me now whenever I bake and cook for my own children.

On many days, it was a special neighbour up the street from me, Agnes Bates, that would call my mom asking for me. She and her husband Emmett had ten children and had been very successful in getting them all ready for life. With love and determination, Agnes and

Emmett got all them through school, and each one of them went on to university and successful careers, no small feat in the day on a single coal miner's salary. Later in life, when Agnes and Emmett were empty nesters, I was finding myself being called upon to run to the store more often. After doing this for a couple of years, Emmett would unexpectedly pass away, leaving Agnes a widow. After the funeral Martin, one of her sons, spoke to my mom asking if I would keep an eye on her and help when needed, with all them now grown and with families of their own and moved away she would need the help. I had no problem with this, and so I became her runner for around ten years, until I moved away and joined the army. I would shovel her driveway, cut the kindling, take out the ashes, cut the grass, and paint in the summer for her. When she ran short on bread or milk, she would call Mom asked for me to run to Buddy Graham's store and pick a few things up for her. Agnes and I became fast friends, and she relied on me more as the years passed.

Going to the store was a great educator in and of itself. The simple act of going to the store for all the neighbourhood did so much to teach me self discipline and practical skills, which I would use throughout my life and military career. Agnes would call my mother and ask if I was around, and if so could Mom send me up to her place to run to the store for her. I would run over, knocking in her door, and she would call me in and hand me the list of things to pick up, knowing what brand she wanted, and what type of milk, so I had to be able to recognize and know what to choose while at the store. Then, there was the counting of money, she would give me a few dollars for the things I would pick up, and I would run up to the store. Once I returned, she would ask me how much it cost and I would tell her, then she would have me count what change I had, and once it matched up, some of the change would be given to me—a dime or quarter. Besides the money, I would come to understand later in life that there were many good lessons to be taken from this experience as the neighbourhood runner.

It's been well over thirty-five years since joining the military and leaving home, and thirty-five years since I've tasted Agnes's cooking. She made the best of homemade cooking and baking, especially during special occasions, such as Christmas and Easter. My scent memory can still recall the smells and aromas from these times in her kitchen. I hold all those memories of my time with Agnes close to my heart, for she was the closest person I ever had to a grandmother, and I loved her as such. But the memories of being welcomed into the Bates family are as close to my mind's eye today, as when I first experienced them.

I remember whenever I would run to the store for her, she would say afterwards, "Come in, Derrick, and I'll make a cup of tea for you." Then, she would say, "How about I make you something to eat?" And as anyone who grew up in Cape Breton knows, you couldn't refuse food, It would be an insult not to at least have a cup of tea and a sandwich.

I think spending time with Agnes served both of us well. With me being one of the youngest of the boys in the neighbourhood I was often left to my own, so I was a kid in need of a friend and Agnes, a widow, in need of company. It was a good fit, and I will be forever grateful for that time and experience in my life. After I would eat supper with her, we would sit in the living room and she would tell stories about growing up as a little girl, stories about politics, and slowly she would open the door to her life to me and it was amazing. I always believe if she had been given the opportunities young women now have, that nothing would have held her back. Unfortunately, she was born in a different time, different era which held women back. But she was much better read in policy and politics than most men I have ever met then and now, she was intelligent, confident, and persuasive when laying out an argument, and I can only imagine how much she could have accomplished in todays society.

She was a nurse in her early life, then a homemaker, worked at a pizza shop then later was a full-time nanny. But throughout all of this, she was a dedicated and loyal mother, grandmother, and friend, who could do whatever was placed before her, as she cared for her ten children and countless grandchildren. I don't think anything was more important than family to Agnes, and I was glad to be included in this group.

Many of the times I would return from running to the store, she would be baking and ask me if I wanted to help. I think this is something many kids are missing today—kitchen time, spending time with your mom, grandma, or a neighbour such as Agnes, is something that teaches lessons far beyond the meal or baked goods. She would have CBC radio on with Peter Gzowski, and would be talking with me, as we would discuss these topics listening to the radio. She was wise, had an incredible knowledge base and taught me many important aspects of listening and persuasive discussion.

She was the master of the kitchen and was a master when it came to cooking and baking. She had her own secret ingredients, and with the years and years of cooking for a big family and all those grand-children, she knew short cuts, how to substitute ingredients if the ones needed weren't there, or how to make something delicious out of seemingly nothing.

When you were a store runner during this time, you were fortunate to interact with so many amazing older people, sharing their wisdom and experiences with me. I was always lucky, because these men and women whom I looked up to, had lived through the great depression, served during the Second World War and they lived in a different time and came through it more resilient and self-reliant. They knew how to adapt and overcome, and those of my generation were the beneficiaries of these experiences.

I think I was lucky to have more "grandparents" than most people. I had access to all their knowledge and lessons to guide me through life. It was a time when everyone in a small coal mining town had a stake in the children, and parents knew when their child went to neighbours' homes, they would be treated as one of their own.

NEW YEAR'S EVE
IN NEW WATERFORD

T HERE WAS A LOT OF FANFARE AROUND NEW YEAR'S EVE IN New Waterford, the excitement that came from knowing that a new year was around the corner, and the wonderment of what it all meant and what was to come in the year ahead. We would have a small supper that afternoon, knowing that there would be another small meal later in the evening, once the clock struck midnight. We would sit around watching Guy Lombardo and his Royal Canadians live from Times Square in New York and wait for the ball to drop. Dad always loved to sit and watch this. I think it reminded him of growing up during the war years, when he was a young man, as this was the music of the day.

Around ten minutes before midnight, and ten minutes after, we would hear shotguns being shot off all around town and wouldn't stop for at least twenty minutes. Meanwhile, we were inside the house watching Guy Lombardo. I always loved to watch the big lighted ball in Times Square slowly coming down. Then his band would play "Auld Lang Syne" as we sang along. Once the New Year had arrived, dad would make his way over next door to the Timmons household next door for his yearly visit, but he was always by himself as was the tradition. You see, it was an old tradition from Scotland called "first footing," where the first person to enter under your threshold in the new year should be tall, dark haired, and bring a few specific gifts. I'm not sure if dad brought these specific things, but he brought a few things with him. He was supposed to bring a small amount of money for good luck and prosperity, some bread to symbolize an abundance of food for the year to come, and a piece of coal or a shot of hard liquor for warmth and happiness.

He enjoyed this yearly visit with our neighbour, Gloria and Adrian. He usually brought over a piece of coal, a loaf of homemade bread, and maybe a beer. We never really had alcohol in the house, so beer had to do for the drink. He felt it was his duty right up until he died, and why not? He began with this in 1959 and continued up until his passing in 1982. Many I tell this story to think it's foolish, just a superstition, but to me it was quaint. It's a little memory and piece of New Waterford, and it expresses beautifully the kindness we shared in our neighbourhood and of what Cape Breton means to me.

While dad was gone next door, mom would have made a potato salad earlier in the day and cut some tomatoes and broil a ham, this was all for a midnight meal while we continued watching Guy Lombardo and his Royal Canadians. We would stay up for hours, until dad finished his visit with the neighbours, then head off to bed. Dad and mom would come upstairs and tuck us in, tell us a bedtime story, my favorite was always "The Big Bad Wolf", then a kiss on the forehead. The year had ended, and we went to sleep with hopes and dreams for the year ahead to come, full of optimism that it would be a little better than the one just passed.

New Year's Day, and we would be up early and off to St. Agnes Church for the New Year's Day Mass, to pray for the very best in the year to come, then back home. Mostly, I remember getting up and watching all the New Year's Day Parades and American football games, I especially remember the Tournament of Roses Parade. My children cannot imagine it when I tell them we watched the parade in black and white. Many children of today have never seen black and white movies or TV, but for us kids and our parents, we would all sit in front of the black and white RCA tube television and watch the parade for hours. Of course, the narrators would remind us of the work it took on the weeks leading up to the parade, mention how every float had to be made with flowers, either crushed or dehydrated flowers and of course we would marvel at this fact, but only imagine all the beautiful colors described to us which we couldn't see with our old black and white TV's.

It wouldn't be until the late seventies when we would get our first color TV and begin to enjoy the parades in the colors we had heard describes years earlier. No matter black and white or color, it's just a blessing that I have these memories with mom, dad, brothers and sisters.

The day would be half over and suddenly it was supper time and another nice holiday meal by mom. This time, hot turkey sandwiches with gravy and homemade French fries to finish off the Christmas turkey. Then, we got our snowsuits on and went outside for awhile to play with all the other kids in the neighbourhood, compare what each other got for Christmas, admire new toboggans, sleds, and toys. Suddenly, in the blink of an eye, the day was done and the freshness of the New Year's celebrations were over until next December 31st. For now, it was off to bed and we would awake tomorrow, to begin anew writing the story for the year ahead.

Dad once told me this quote from John Wayne, "Tomorrow hopes we have learned something from yesterday." I didn't quite understand this for the longest time, but finally, as I moved into my twenties and began my own life, I slowly understood. I believe it means that we cannot allow ourselves to be prisoners to our mistakes, failures, and shortcomings of the past, that we must approach each day in the now, as a clean slate full of optimism and promise. Took me a long time to come to this understanding, but I did, and now every New Year's Eve, I gently remind myself that I can afford to have self-forgiveness for last year's shortcomings and start anew the new year ahead.

I think the days leading up to, and shortly after the new year allows us to be nostalgic, to look back at what means the most to us, to give us a glimpse into what we need to do to rekindle those magical moments in our lives with friends, family, and ourselves. Paradoxically, looking to the new year in this way will help us to do better in the year ahead, help us to achieve our goals, and remind us of what's important and what got us to where we are today. We see ourselves, our goodness, our strength to put one foot in front of the other and move forward.

NIGHTCRAWLER HUNTERS

WAS SITTING HERE AT MY HOME, LOOKING AT SOME OLD PICTURES and came across one of my neighbour Bobby. I remember when I was a very little boy, he was one of my first heroes growing up in my little world of Heelan Street. I still remember when Bobby had a Honda motorbike, I was only 7 or so and he took me for my first ride on a bike. I still remember it was an old 4-stroke and the engine made this tinging sound when Bobby gave it a little gas. It was a beautiful little bike, red with white pinstripes and a white leather seat. With his help, I got onto the back of the bike and hung on to his waist as tight as I could as he drove around the block, very slow, but to me it might as well have been 100 MPH. Later in life Bobby would get married and leave home for work in Toronto, and it would be only on his summer vacations when he would come home, for a week-long vacation with his family, that I would get to see him. Later in the early 80's, he would return to New Waterford for good. He began visiting our house every morning during that first summer, he would come over when mom was sitting on the front veranda, they would spend hours there, talking and drinking tea, "joking and smoking," as we'd call it.

One summer's day, Bobby told me of a way to make some money. He told me that I should start a worm business and it would be easy. All I had to do was catch nightcrawlers and put a sign up on the front fence and sell them for fifty cents a dozen. I figured that this would be an easy way to make a few dollars. Myself, I had never done much catching of worms before, but he explained it to me. Later that night, I went out with my flashlight and pointed it at the ground, but as I scanned with the light back and forth, there were no nightcrawlers on the grass to be found. All I could see were these slime trails left behind from where they were earlier. I knew there were a lot of nightcrawlers there, because every time it rained they would be all over our front sidewalk and it would be impossible not to walk on them. So, why couldn't I find any in my front yard?

The next day, when Bobby came over and was talking with mom, I went and asked him why there were no worms last night. He asked, "Derrick, did you put some water on the grass an hour or so before you went looking, and did you filter the light from your flashlight?" I told him "no", and he said that when it got dark out later that evening, he would come over and show me how it was done.

To his word, later in the evening after supper, Bobby came over and of course he had a story for everything he did. He told me that the nightcrawlers were very smart creatures, and that you had to outsmart them to persuade them out of their holes. He told me that first, we had to put lots of water on the front yard, so I put the sprinkler on the front yard and let it run for a half hour or so. Bobby told me that they would be tricked into thinking it was raining out, and they would leave their holes, and when they came to the surface, they would lay almost all the way out of the ground.

Next, Bobby told me that nightcrawlers were smart and would warn each other as to what was going on in their neighborhood, so you had to be careful, when you walked on the grass to only slide your feet along the grass and gently place it down, or they would feel the vibrations and scurry back into their holes. Also, another problem with catching them was the light; he told me that I needed to cup my hand over the flashlight and only leave a little filter out through my fingers, and that this would be enough light to see them. The final part of the worm hunt would be the catching of them. Again, Bobby told me that they were so smart that if you approached them head on, they would feel your presence and pull back into the hole. So, the trick was to get them from behind.

So, we began after dark, with the ground still wet with dew. I pounced on the first one I saw and began pulling on it, and heard a 'snap.' It broke in half as I tried to pull it from its slimy earth home. So here I was, holding half a worm and it had its guts squeezed out of it running down my fingers, I was a little disgusted, but Bobby told me this was the dangers of nightcrawler hunting. Another teaching point from Bobby was, "You don't pull the worm out in one motion, Derrick, you pull, then when you feel him grabbing and pulling back into the hole, you relax letting him think your letting go, and just when he feels your grip relax to let him go, you will feel him relax as he prepares to go back in the hole, then this is where you pull him straight out." Wow, I thought. There's a lot of tricks you need to know to catch nightcrawlers. We must have been out in my front yard for hours catching a couple dozen nightcrawlers. Meanwhile mom was sitting on the veranda talking occasionally to Bobby and laughing at our shenanigans.

I recall how we laughed so much that night in my front yard as we caught so many slimy nightcrawlers. However, in the end it never mattered how many I had caught, I wasn't much of a salesman, as I would soon find out, and never actually sold any. However, Bobby felt sorry for me and took me fishing and onto another adventure down at the shore at the breakwater a couple of days later. For myself, many of these experiences growing up, were never really about the activity I was doing, rather it was more so in the lessons you would take away from these times and the fun you had making the memories.

NO. 12 COLLIERY WASHHOUSE

W HEN I WAS A KID GROWING UP, WE DID NOT HAVE A shower at our home nor a water heater either. With my dad working at No. 12 Colliery, as with all miners, he could take us to the washhouse for a shower as long as it was in between shifts and we were with him, but we had to go right in, get a shower, and leave immediately afterwards.

One winter, there was a storm just finishing and the winds were still gusting, we were walking down West Ave heading to the washhouse for a shower, it was a very cold and windy winter day. I was only five or six, and my dad held my hand as the wind was blowing and taking my breath away. My brother Kim, two years older than I, had placed a scarf over his face so he wasn't having the same issues as me. It seemed to last forever that walk from our home on Heelan Street to the Washhouse.

Once we got there, I was almost in tears. It had taken forever to get there or, at least that's how it felt to me as a five-year-old. As we entered the washhouse, I was hit immediately with the heat that the giant boiler pumped throughout the building. To my front, there were benches against all the walls, where miners would sit, waiting for the coal cars to come up from underground. There was a pop machine that had the coldest and best tasting pop I could ever imagine, and we knew that after we got a shower, dad would put a quarter in the machine, and my brother and I would each get a pop. I almost always chose Iron Brew, but sometimes a cream soda would be in order. Next to the pop machine was a ramp that led up to these two big doors and into the main washhouse. Once dad opened them and I looked inside, it was wonderful. Every time I went with dad and my brother over to the washhouse there was always something new that caught my eye, I felt like I was getting to see a little of my father's work life.

We would arrive every Saturday morning for a shower, and there were also other fathers arriving there at the same time with their boys. We would get undressed and run into the shower room, looking down the long shower area there were about two hundred shower heads, it was gigantic and the water was extra hot coming directly from the broiler room next door, we had to be careful not to go directly under the shower until we had it adjusted properly. Then we would begin with the washing of our faces, arms, legs, but help each other out by washing each other's backs. When I tell people of my experiences growing up and going to the washhouse, at times I get a raised eyebrow. I guess to many unacquainted with Cape Breton coal miners and their families' lives, they might think it strange. But the washhouse I think served not only as a place to wash the dirt and dust of the day off, but it was essentially a place where the men would joke around, pull pranks on one another like hiding another's towel while they were in the shower, talk about family and what they were looking forward to with summers vacation around the corner. It was a place of community, respect, and well being.

The building itself didn't seem to end. The first room was about a football field long, and off to the left side was the lamp house, where the miners would get their lamps. There was another room with danger signs on it, and it was hot and steam coming from a pipe by the gigantic boiler, which produced the hot water for the two hundred shower heads. Next to this was the bathroom, with eight or so toilets and a urinal trough, which up to ten people could use at a time. At the end of this first room was a wall with a double entrance into it, and behind here was another football-field-sized room.

The high ceilings seemed to touch the sky and had all these clothes on hooks up towards the ceiling on a rope and pulley system. Some had round, wire baskets, where the men could put their wallets and cigarettes. Work clothes hung in the washhouse on these ropes, and at the beginning of the shift, the miners would hang their clean clothes on the hooks for safe keeping, and then put on their dirty, damp pit clothes, full of sweat and coal dust, and tighten up their thick pit belts and put on their steel toed boots. Once dressed, they would then pull up their clean clothes to the ceiling for safe keeping. Funny thing is, I can never remember ever hearing of the theft of anyone's money or personal belongings from these hook and pulley systems. I believe the brotherhood they all shared, knowing that at any moment a cave in or fire could end their lives, created a trust amongst one another that was more important than rifling through another's belongings, a lesson we could use today. At the end of the shift, the reverse would happen when they would take of their damp, wet and dirty pit clothes then pull them up to the ceiling overnight.

As a child, I didn't understand the need for those hooks and baskets. But in the belly of the mine, it is cold, wet, and dirty, not something you want to take home to your family every night. Coming out of the mine in this state, then having the luxury of getting a hot shower and a bar soap, afforded to these men what we called in the military call *esprit de corps*, or a common sense of pride.

All the while of getting clean, the miners would share stories about family, or what the day's work was about. I heard of animated arguments about miners' favorite hockey teams, or maybe the shift before changing one or two miners' clothes, so there would be a bit of confusion after a shift, not done in meanness, but as a prank, and it was always taken lightly. I remember being with my dad and him talking to his friends and talking about things I knew nothing about and laughing as they had a chew of tobacco or a cigarette, while I sat on the bench and drank my Iron Brew pop, listening to these men tell their stories and the spontaneous hardy laughter which would occasionally erupt.

When dad finally got home after work, the only trace we would see of him having worked twelve miles underground were those distinctive coal dust rings around his eyes. But even these little rings around his eyes were enough to remind us the work he did was dangerous, and every day when he walked through the door was another day lady luck was with us, and the rings around his eyes a subtle reminder that we would have to give dad up again the next day for another shift in the bowels of the earth.

We eventually got a hot water tank, but continued going to the mine until it closed after the fire in 1973. After this, on occasion, we would venture out to Lingan Mine for a shower, but it would never feel the same as growing up with No. 12 Colliery next door to us.

PARENTS
PRAGMATISM

REMEMBER ONE DAY, MY FATHER TELLING ME A STORY ABOUT WHEN he was on shift at No. 12 Colliery. As he was recalling the story, he was smiling and laughing, he told me about a machine that they used in the coalmine, dad said it was used in longwall mining and was called, a Dosco Continuous Miner. It was a machine which had thousands of diamond teeth, that would chew up the wall face as it went back and forth across the face of the coal seam, sending the coal back on a conveyer belt, where it would eventually be loaded on coal cars and sent to the surface. Dad told me the miners had nicknamed it "the pig," because it could "eat" so much coal off the coal face at a time.

So, on this one shift, the pig broke down, and that management sent down a couple young engineers who were there for work experience that summer. The engineers were busy writing things down, talking to each other back and forth, and punching in numbers on their calculators. However, they still couldn't figure out why it wouldn't work. My dad went on to tell me that an older coal miner was watching, and had worked with the machine for years said to the young engineers, "If you take that rod from over there, and put it here, and move that wire over there, that should make it work." Seeing they had nothing to lose, they followed the old miner's directions, and suddenly the machine started. The reality was in the miners knowing the machines from working day in and day out with them, his practical knowledge of the working environment that a formal education could have never provided, and it allowed the coal miners to problem solve on their feet.

I saw this thinking-on-your-feet approach everywhere. I know what I learned from watching these men, it was that I could do what was needed to fix things around the house and be self reliant. I don't remember so many roofing companies back then as I do now. Doing a roof was talked about on shift maybe, or a few of the neighbours got together and talked about it, planned it, and then did it themselves, either on a weekend or during miners' summer vacation. They were practical and able to do most anything, with support from their friends.

There was so many people around town when I was a kid who had what were called "foot gardens" or "victory gardens," which were very popular during WWI and WWII, when people across Canada were encouraged to plant vegetables for personal use, to free up other resources for the war effort. I saw some of these, as there were still some around town with the older people planting gardens every spring when I was growing up. What it showed me was that these people were self reliant and able to feed themselves during the summer season and into fall. I still remember my neighbours at the end of every summer making chow and relish from summer garden vegetables and making preserves out of them, a practice seldom seen today, with the availability and wastage of food we often witness.

I also don't recall seeing too many plumbers or carpenters, as most men did their own work. I think that there was an wealth of practicality in these men and women, I believe it was *because* of these times, with only the fathers working outside the homes and money wasn't in great abundance, that there was a need for this practicality. One time, when we were having problems with the fuse box coming into the house off the main power pole outside. I had just arrived home from playing outside and called for mom when I came in. "mom! mom!" I called.

And then I heard, "I'm up here, Derrick." She was calling from the bathroom, where the power came into the house and into the fuse box. These were live wires coming into the home, directly off the electrical pole and mom thought nothing of it. It needed to be done and we couldn't afford to hire an electrician, so here she was, with the screwdrivers and plyers and about an hour later she was done, a new fuse box was in. Even today, I think of what terrible outcomes could have happened, but luckily, they didn't. For years after, when I would tell this story to mom's friends, we would laugh at those antics and the risks that she took at the time.

If we think about our lives today, how many of us can fix our own cars, do our own carpentry, or grow and bake our own food? Once again out of necessity, most of the men then could take apart the carburetor, replace the seals, and put it back together again. Most of the women I used to run to the store for, could substitute ingredients on the fly and still make an awesome, delicious pie, with a little adjustment. It was a practicality during this time, that somehow, our modern life with its conveniences, has since washed away. We now find everywhere pre-made food and pre-measured baking products, no more from scratch meals or baking. No, we are told time is too important for that, so it's left to food companies to do for us. Funny thing I have noticed is the more conveniences we get, the more computer and gadgets, the easier it becomes, we somehow have less and less time for one another, for conversation, or to just sit and be still. I sometimes wish I could go back, if only for a day.

PARAMOUNT
THEATRE

WAS THINKING THE OTHER DAY ABOUT THE OLD PARAMOUNT theatre in New Waterford after reading an article on its current use as the Urban Centre for town. I then thought back to when I was a kid and how the downtown was populated in the 1960's and 70's with buildings and businesses everywhere, from one end of Plummer Ave at Heelan St to the other end at King St. In my mind, I can evoke memories of looking around at these places, as we would walk to the theatre on a Saturday afternoon to see a show. The local theatre was owned by Harry Gregor and his brother Fred, who operated the Paramount Theatre from the 60's until its closing in the mid 80's. Myself, I began going to movies at the Paramount from the time I was around five and continued until I finished high school in the early 80's. I recall at the time when I first began going, money wasn't in abundance for most coal mining families and most times mom would give, Kim and I just enough to get in to a show and maybe a bag of popcorn, which we appreciated because we knew she had little to give us. However, there were occasions where she couldn't give us the cost of admission, so we were left to our own devices to figure out how to make a couple of dollars to go or not.

My brother and I would begin a few days prior to the weekend figuring our ways to make a couple of dollars so we could go to the show. The show was only .75 cents or so in the late 60's and for another .50 cents you could get your fountain pop and popcorn. I remember one time where we collected a pile of old wood from around the neighborhood and my brother cut it up with a bow saw while I took the hatchet and made piles of kindling for started wood. We would then tie them in bundles and go around the neighbourhood selling it for .25 cents a bundle. Enough of the neighbours would buy it from us and made a few dollars, enough that if we split the money we would be able to go and see the show. Later in the year, as winter arrived, we would shovel driveways to raise funds for the show, I found it was always easier to find a driveway to shovel in winter then to find someone to buy our kindling.

I recall on occasion one of the guys not having enough to go to the show and began to walk away with his head down, one of the older boys would stop him and we would all chip in the extra few nickels and dimes we had so that we all could go and no one was ever left behind. These were the lessons of childhood which we were grounded in, take care of your friends, and never ever leave anyone behind. Even once at the show, if we sensed one of us didn't have enough for a treat, we would share ours with them, it always seemingly worked out for us.

I used to go to the Saturday Matinee and I recall when there was a good kid's movie showing, especially a double feature with the cartoon shorts at the beginning, the line would be from the door of the theatre along the railing in front of the post office up to the corner of Smith St and Plummer Ave. We would slowly shuffle our way down until it was our turn and we had made it up to the front doors. Inside the doors, there was a booth with a glass window and a little hole to pass the money through at the bottom. Once you paid there were little metal slots even with the top of the metal table where the ticket would pop out from once you paid. The lady behind the window took the money from the little round opening at the bottom of the glass.

Once I got my ticket I went into the theatre and up the four stairs leading to the mezzanine which was where the concession stand was for popcorn, licorice, and fountain pop. As you walked in the scents of all this deliciousness would assault your senses. At the top of the stairs stood an usher, whose name was Neil I believe, he would take the ticket then tear it in half giving half a stub back to us. The bathrooms were over in the far corner, this was during the time when people still smoked in public buildings, so there were always a lot of people by the bathroom corner getting their last puff of a cigarette in before the show.

I think the theatre sat at least 700 people, or more, and on matinee days every single seat would be occupied. I remember the spring-loaded seats which would lay flat when you sat on them and pop up vertically one you stood up. I would come up to the row with my brother, then pick out a seat and put my bum on the top of the seat and let my weight slowly go down and the seat would flip forward and go flat, then sitting down there would be a soft velour covers seat awaiting me, which I would enthusiastically sink into and wiggle around getting myself comfortable.

There would be that sweet smell of buttered popcorn rising from the bucket on my lap, I could feel my feet sticking to the floor as I picked up and placed down each foot, from fountain pop spilt the evening before, it was always a little laugh but soon we moved onto other things. I usually liked to arrive a little early, that way I could get my treats and find a good seat, usually around halfway back in the middle so we could get the best view of the screen. There would be many familiar faces from our St Agnes school and around the neighbourhood who had the same idea as we had to come see a show. It was exciting looking around the theatre seeing some young teenage boys with first awkward attempts at courting their little girlfriends with them, giggling and laughing as they were having their first date, and I remember the distinct buzz in the theatre, with all the talking and excitement all around, there was pure anticipation for everyone waiting for the show to begin.

Once I got my bearing I would begin shoving my popcorn by the fistfuls into my mouth and wait until the curtains were pulled back, we knew this was going to happen soon because the light would go dim then bright, a couple of times beforehand, then a silence would come over the crowd. You could feel the excitement, the low drone of kids talking and giggling quietly as the clock on the wall slowly ticked towards show time. As the lights went down we would all clap and cheer just before the movie was to begin. As the show began, we quickly rallied around the good guy, every now and then when the villain was winning, boo's would be loudly heard and some time empty popcorn boxes would be thrown towards the screen, but as the hero gained the upper hand, a roar of cheers would take over as the bad guy, good guy struggle was ongoing. Fun times in my memory banks of these days.

I remember one of my first movies it was "Chitty Chitty Bang Bang" with Dick Van Dyke, then "Herbie the Love bug", as well as a badly dubbed version of Bruce Lee's "Enter the Dragon", where the voiced over would be heard then with a slight delay, his lips would be moving with no sound, then sound with no movement, it was funny. But in the end no matter what movie was being played, it was all fun and the fun didn't stop after the movie. We would pour out onto the street at four in the afternoon wrestling and rolling around on the grass between the Paramount and the Post Office, this continued all the way home with all us kids play fighting all the way.

Later In high school, I would help a friend from school change the Marquee sign every few days when a new movie would come to town. He did this as a part time job while going to school and part of the deal was that he could get in for free to the movies, better yet take one friend with him if he wanted, so he was nice enough to include me a couple of times when I would assist him with the changing of the marquee sign. All I had to worry about then was my popcorn and fountain pop. I attended my last movie there around 1977 or 78 and it was "Pete's Dragon". I think it closed in the mid 80's, then it was sold to the town to be used as a Pensioners hall, social work offices and the towns library. Its sad to see the repurposing of buildings happen in a community, but at least the old theatre was spared, unlike so many other beautiful buildings with their architecture now gone forever, and the newer generation never to be seen or experienced. Perhaps this is just the way life is, times change, tastes change and so we move on, but the memories we made in the old Paramount Theatre all those years ago will never leave us.

RED ROVER, RED ROVER, SEND GARY RIGHT OVER!

GROWING UP, I USED TO GO TO THE FIELD OFF MARY AVENUE, behind the Gillis's house. There were so many kids there every afternoon and night during the summer. I would follow my older brother Kim, the boys he hung around with, and so many others use to gather there as well. Much of the time would be spent playing kick the can, skipping, or my favorite, Red Rover, where you could clothesline your opponent as they tried to breach your line of locked arms.

We would have two opposing teams across the field from one another, and one of the older boys on the other team would shout, "Red rover, red rover, send Derrick right over!" I would quickly look at the line up across from me and see where the weakest link would be and charge forward, trying to break through. If we didn't, then we became part of the opposing team, and if we broke through, we went back to our side. It was all in fun, but I remember having the bruises after this game.

We also wrestled almost every night. We even had championship belts, and would win them, taking them home for the night, and talk about it as if we were really winning a world title. It was the time where Atlantic Grand Prix Wrestling was on TV and had characters like Freddie Sweetan and Killer Karl Krupp, and of course, Stephan Petipas, who usually always won over the competition, though occasionally the Cuban Assassin would take a win. They would travel all over the

Atlantic provinces during the summer. We would all watch it on TV every Saturday afternoon, then at night, when we met at the field off Mary Avenue again, we would toss each other around, play fighting and pretending to be these guys, trying to talk like them and make up wrestling scenarios.

It was always fun, and hardly anyone ever got hurt, until one night! I was wrestling, when suddenly thrown on my back and one of the older boys jumped, pretending he was going to land on me and give me the elbow to the chest, however he made an error in estimating the distance and landed on my outstretched arm, breaking my wrist and radius in half. After this little accident, there was a timeout for all of us from wrestling, once the moms got wind of our activities. I guess I was never destined to win the "World Tag Team" title.

We would also play Kick the Can some evenings in the field behind MacDonald's Hardware. It was a simple game, where everyone took their turn being "it," and we would make a circle with chalk, or dig our heel in the ground and scratch out a circle, and put an old tin can in the middle. Then you would hide your eyes and count to ten or twenty while everyone scattered and hid all over the neighbourhood.

Then, you would say, "Ready or not, here I come!" and then whoever was "it" began running around, trying to catch everyone hiding, and tagging them. Then, they would have to go into the circle. You would try to find everyone before someone would sneak up behind you, running through the circle and kicking the can, thereby "freeing" those that you had caught. This was fun, but I found we only did this a couple of times, before it quickly lost steam, and we would move onto another game, where we could be more in motion.

There was another game called "Peggy" that we use to play as well, where you would have a six-inch piece of wood, tapered at both ends, and a long stick or willow branch. I remember playing this on Second Street with David, Raymond, Eugene, and my brother, Kim. We would all take a turn to hit the "Peggy", it was placed over a shallow hole and then we would flip it up, and when it got to where we could hit it, we hit it with the willow branch to see how far it could go.

It was little like baseball and a little like cricket, in that your had three swings, and you would then pace off from the starting point to where it landed after three attempts. The one with the most paces won. A simple game, but we played it for hours.

From the time, the last bell rang in June, until the first one rang again in September, we would be gone all day. Wake up, eat quickly and then gone. Unlike today's "social outing," meaning emailing and texting one another, our social outings meant walking out to the pump house by Waterford Lake for a swim, or taking my banana bike to meet all my friends and spend the day riding and laughing with an old hockey card in the spokes. We were all trained to occasionally call our moms and let them know where we were, or ask if it was ok to eat over at your friends.

Then, there would be the Tasty Treat Truck with the tinny-sounding circus music, and suddenly a quiet street would become a beehive of activity, with kids pouring out of every corner of the neighbourhood.

It would be fun all day and into the evening when either your Mom would scream out looking for us or the 8:30 air raid siren would scream out across town telling the kids to get home and off the street. We all knew to get home once we heard this and to not test the waters or you would get a good slap on the backside and told not to be late again.

These were our summers growing up, unscheduled, with no organized activities, for the most part. If today's parents and politicians saw how we were raised back then, I would venture a guess that most of our parents would be in jail for being unfit parents and leaving us play unsupervised. Looking back at my youth and at these times with little supervision, it was the best of times to be a kid. We were the beneficiaries of free-range parenting, I guess you'd call it?

SHOOTING THE DRAG

When I finished my first year in high school at Breton Education Centre, as a teenager I couldn't wait to take my place downtown on the Main Street, Plummer Ave, with my friends. Downtown was the place everyone wanted to be when I was a teenager in the seventies and eighties. It was a rite of passage, and everyone who had ever lived in New Waterford, Glace Bay or Sydney went through it. That first summer I began hanging down on Plummer Ave, it was a diverse mix of kids, from grades nine to twelve. Then, there were those older people, finished school, maybe in college or university, who still hung around the main drag and thought they were young enough to be with the high school crowd. Regardless, it was an amazing time for us all.

For most of us, the preparations for the evening began back at home, around five o'clock, with getting the clothes out that you would wear for the evening, the perfect jeans, t-shirt, jean jacket, and sneakers; it had to be just right. Then there was the preening, getting washed, brushing teeth, smelling your breath, brushing them again and blow into your hand, and brushing again until you thought it was right. Then, the matter of combing hair then parting it in the middle for us guys, and the girls with that Farrah Fawcett flip. And this was just the getting ready!

When the time to get dressed arrived, it wasn't as simple as putting on those jeans and shirt you had earlier laid out. As soon as you put them on you would think "no, those jeans aren't right", then try on another pair. Those were too tight. The next pair, too baggy. Then, after forty-five frustrating minutes, you would try on the first pair you had picked earlier in the day and realize they were just right. Then, you would make a few phone calls and rally your friends to a meeting point, usually in front of the post office. All the while, you had on the radio, listening to CJCB or CHER and the music of the day, getting pumped up for the night ahead.

On my way downtown, I would stop by and see Gary and Keith, and if they were going out, then stop at Buddy Graham's, and buy a pack a gum and some loose cigarettes. Along the way, you could smell the summer breeze in the air, as you turned the corner of Woolworth's, you were facing Plummer Avenue, cars would be coming up the street and turning around on Baker Street up towards the New Waterford Bowling Alleys, then those same cars heading back down the main drag, it seemed as if there were people everywhere, on the benches in the park, by Hinchey's Grocery Store, walking by the legion and credit union, sitting on the old, concrete foundation across from Schwartz Clothing.

My destination was the post office, to lean on railing. Next to here was the Paramount Theatre, with its double-header show on a Friday night. The railing in front of the post office went the full length of the property; it was here where the bulk of teenagers would sit, stand, and just hang out. It was packed from end to end. Then, there was the crowd out in front of Harry Yip's corner store, and another group would be down at Cookie McLeod's pool hall, and there was yet another group up the other end by the Davis Park. All these groups coexisted and often would stay within their own areas along the main drag.

It was cool, when you think of it, all the teenagers in town would be on or around the Main Street, and the police knew where we were. It was great, with the guys in their muscle cars bombing up and down the street, there were Super Bees, Dusters, Camaros. It seemed they were everywhere, beautiful muscle cars shooting the drag all night long.

At exactly eight thirty every night, the old air raid siren would go off. It would be heard everywhere in town and there would be no one who hadn't heard it. This was the warning for kids under sixteen to get off the streets and go home. If you were under sixteen, you could be in your own yard or close by, but not downtown or out roaming around after this. In New Waterford, this practice has a storied history, and I believe continues today. This would begin the start of the first wave of people walking home from downtown and heading home. It would take mostly those under 16 years old away, but there was still lots going on down on Plummer and with it only being eight thirty, there was still another few hours to go.

There would be the young guys courting their first girlfriends, walking up to the park at one end of the street, then making their way back, up and down the main street all night, talking about nothing, and yet talking about everything. Later, they might go to the pizza shop or to Simeon's for a plate of French fries. That's often how the night would end up, a plate of chips at eleven thirty or so, then it would be that long walk home. The police would start shooing people off the streets and gently sending us on our way.

We were never quite finished, because usually on the way home, if I was with Keith or Gary, I would stop by their place. Their mom and dad would still be up sitting in the kitchen and the kettle would be warmed for a cup of tea and a cookie, before finally heading home. We would then settle in for a couple of hours, of either just talking in the front room or in the kitchen, having a tea and playing game after game of cribbage.

After my night downtown on Plummer Ave, it would be close to one in the morning by the time I got home, I would often be coming down the walkway in front of our home in Heelan Street to find mom sitting on the veranda waiting for me. Cape Breton moms always seemed to have their radar on, knowing what was going on with their kids, where they were and if they were safe or in danger. Usually when I got home, mom would be sitting there and ask me how the night was, dad was usually on backshift at the mine as she waited up for me. She would tell me to put on the kettle and make her a cup of tea, then she would roll up a couple of cigarettes on the front veranda with the loose tobacco and Export papers. Then with our tea, we would then sit on the veranda enjoying the beautiful summers night, the smell of the fresh cool air and of the trees everywhere, talking the night gently away until it was time for me to head to bed.

SKATING AT
THE RINK

Y FIRST RECOLLECTION OF SKATING AS A CHILD WAS AT THE St. Agnes outdoor skating rink when I was at about six or seven years old. The rink was located between the old, three-storey St. Agnes Elementary School, which I first attended in 1966, and St. Agnes Convent. I believe it was Father Frank Morley who was the Parish Priest there at the time, and it was a few years prior to the community rink being built in 1973. During these times, the communities that were located around town close to the churches, would have these outdoor rinks provided for kids and their families.

Ours was a regulation rink with sideboards, and it was illuminated with 100-watt lightbulbs, strung on wires, which were nailed onto high on two-by-fours around the oval rink. At the end of the rink, was a big door with a heavy latch that was opened, you could enter and exit as you pleased while skating. The changing room was the school basement across the way.

I began skating at the St. Agnes outdoor rink, between the convent and old, three-story elementary school (which later became the Kinsman Boxing Club) as a child, skating in circles to the "Skaters Waltz," which was blaring through the old, trumpet-shaped, and tin-sounding speakers. I still remember this as if it were yesterday.

We would show up early on most occasions, except when it was the adult skating and as kids knew we weren't allowed on the ice. On the sound system, a Sonny James record would be playing, "Young Love." I can still feel the cold air on my face as the adults passed us, they would be skating in a rhythmical motion, almost like a military marching band, with the beat of the song. Left skate, right skate, left skate, and on, and on. They were beautiful skaters to watch, mesmerizing me with their rhythm, seemingly so effortless, each push of their blades.

You paid your quarter at the entrance to get in. As you were going in, they had Q-tips that they dipped into alcohol, I believe. They would put an X on the top of your hand with the Q-tip, then when you came out of the changing room, they would get you to put your hand under a black light and it would glow, we were mesmerized with this and didn't understand how they made it glow. Down the basement was a long stairway to what was the foyer towards the gym, and it was here that they had benches set up for us to change into our skates, then we would slide our boots under the benches. As usual, I would try to tighten up my wax covered laces, but could never get them tight enough, so I asked one of the older boys there if he could help, and he said sure, and while doing this, he tried to explain to me the best way to tie up my skates, so next time I could be a little more independent.

We then made our way upstairs, and watched the adults as they finished. Once they finished, it was the kids' turn to skate. There were no such things as Zamboni's at the time so everything during these times was done manually. So, before we could go on the ice, some of the older boys and men would jump on the ice and skate around the rink with big snow shovels, pushing off all the snow the skaters had created, and making it ready for us. We would then hop onto the ice and skate around with our coats, toques, and mittens on. Once again, they would put on the old, scratched recording of the Skaters Waltz, as it would blare out from the speakers we would begin skating around in circles. Most of us were only seven or eight years old. There were a few parents with the smaller kids, who had bob-skates on over their boots and confined themselves to the centre of the ice, slipping and sliding around, while we would try skating around the outer perimeter. Then, of course, there were the older boys and girls, who were much more confident,

I never had a brand-new pair of skates for myself, I think my first pair were from one of the bags of hand-me-downs, tube skates with leather uppers. Thinking back, they were very old and worn with little metal left on the blade from sharpening, but to me as a child, they were as good as anything new. I was a bit nervous, so as I skated around the rink I hung close to the side boards, on wobbly ankles and occasionally would slip as the teenagers zipped by me unexpectedly.

As I tried skating. I would fall, get up, fall again, and repeat this most of the night. By halfway through the night, my hands and cheeks would be cold, nevertheless I would keep on going around and around. At the halfway point of the skate there would be an announcement and we would be told to change direction. Half of the time was clockwise, the other half counter-clockwise. It was a good hour and a half when time was up, and by then we were played out and tired.

As we headed back into the basement of the school on our skates, we could feel a wall of heat coming from the change room hitting our faces, then we would feel the warmth slowly returning to our cheeks, as we took off our skates and put on our winter boots. Although tired from the long night of skating, we were content and happy with the evening and knew it was time to go home.

As we were leaving, the men were finishing clearing the snow off the ice and were flooding it for the next day. We made our way back home, where we would have a hot drink and maybe a cookie and then go off to bed, after brushing our teeth, for a good night's sleep. Off to bed to dream about heading back to St. Agnes rink the next day and doing it all again.

As the years passed, the community was growing and began to want an indoor rink, so in the early seventies, the greater New Waterford community came together through donations, fund raising, and check offs by the town's coal miners, built the New Waterford Community Center up by BEC on Victoria Avenue. I remember, when it first opened, how the community embraced having this new facility and the excitement it brought. I remember my first time entering the rink. The first thing which struck me was the newness of the rink, smell of freshly painted seats and boards, the sting of the cold air as it hit my face and the odour of ammonia in the air from the ice making machine. There was a light fog, slightly above the ice, so clean and shiny, just waiting there for us kids to carve it up with our skates. Everything was so pristine, you could see the hard work and dedication which the maintenance team had put into getting it ready.

While it wasn't the same feeling as being outdoors on the old St. Agnes rink, this one somehow felt special going in there for my first time. It was during this time of going into the new Community Center indoor rink, I decided to experiment and began skating barefoot in my skates. I found the contact with the leather and tightness around my foot felt better, and I could feel every time I pushed off when the blade cut into the ice. I loved sitting on the seats and lacing up. Taking off my socks and tucking them into my boots, sliding my bare feet into the skate and then starting at the bottom, tightening the lace each time it was pulled through the eye holes, all the way up to the top of the skate, until they felt snug and just right. Sometimes, I would stop halfway through the two-hour skate and take them off for a minute, and then go through the whole procedure of tightening them up again.

Kids would come on and off the ice at their own leisure. There were the "rink rats," who policed the ice and caught the kids who were skating too fast, or zipping in and out of the other kids as they nervously skated along. They would be the young lovers, a first date, arm in arm as they skated in rhythm to the music for hours. During the evening, some would put on hard-plastic blade protectors to walk over to the washrooms or canteen, but for me there was enough rubber matting around the rink, that this wasn't necessary. I looked forward every Friday to going to the canteen and the hot dogs you could buy here, with the freshly steamed buns kept in a glass steamer box. This, along with a hot chocolate, seemed to top off the outing at the rink for my Friday night.

Once the big doors opened at the end of the rink and we heard the Zamboni start up, we knew it was time to get off the ice. There would be a flurry of activity, with the rink rats hopping on the ice and going along the side of the boards, pushing the ice shavings out from the base of the boards so the Zamboni could pick them up and leave a nice smooth surface. While this was gong on, all of us kids were busily taking off our skates and putting on our winter boots.

I can't explain it, but there was a feeling of completeness at the end of these nights. We were out for a couple of hours, skating and laughing and joking around, having fun. Leaving the rink, there would always be parents at the door waiting or sitting in their warm cars with the engines running, awaiting their children's arrival for a drive home. As for myself, well I wasn't so lucky to have a car waiting for me and had to walk back the mile towards our home on Heelan Street, yet with the satisfaction of a fun night out with my friends.

SKIPPING SCHOOL— TRUANT OFFICER

I T HAD BEEN A HOT WEEK TOWARDS THE END OF MAY. I WAS IN grade five at St. Agnes Elementary, and I had just left home heading for school. I jumped the fence in the backyard and went across the field on Second Street towards the brook and met up with Charlie and Wayne. As we crossed the field down the hill towards old No. 12 Colliery, we jumped the brook and headed up towards the school. Once we were across the brook, suddenly Charlie had and idea! His idea was to skip school for the day and have fun around town, a much-needed break from school! But we'd have to be careful, for during these times, you would never see kids walking around during school hours. And, if adults saw this they would speak up and ask why you weren't in school.

So, there we were. It was decision time.

Charlie: "Wayne, you in?"

"Yes!"

"Derrick, you in?"

"Yes!"

As I said this, my mind was racing. I'd never skipped school before, and I knew who the Truant Office was, Mr. Bill Copeland, and I had heard that if he caught you skipping school, you would be sent to the boy's school in Shelburne. I had spoken to some of the guys who went there over the years and I didn't like the thought of being sent there for skipping school. I didn't want to do it, but I didn't want to look like I wasn't one of the guys.

Charlie had a pack of Zig Zag tobacco with vogue papers, so we all rolled up a cigarette and started puffing as he lit a match for me. Cough,

cough, cough. This was only the second or third of my early experiences with smoking. I said, "Charlie, I feel weird and kind of dizzy." I got a little nicotine buzz, lightheaded and I didn't feel too good, but I kept smoking because I really wanted to fit in and look cool.

We sat there for awhile, and after a half hour or so when the nicotine buzz wore off, we went exploring along the brook back towards the dam, then over the tracks heading towards the old coal mine explosives bunker. Suddenly out of nowhere, a pit cop caught site of us and the chase began. We took off towards New Waterford Lake area and the pump house. Eventually, we lost him and made it to the pump house, where we stripped down into our underwear and went for a dip. It was great skipping school on a hot day, taking some time off, and go swimming with a couple of friends.

After awhile, when we got tired from swimming, we sat in the sun until we were dried, then dressed and headed back towards the dam and up some side streets to Baker Street, where my Aunt Lucille lived. We were getting hungry now, and she always had cookies. She made us a cup of tea and gave us some cookies and no questions were asked. I was pretty sure she knew we were skipping, but let it go without mentioning it. After this we all thanked her and headed back towards my house and ended up behind J.W. MacDonald's Hardware Store, in the field behind the old barn. Charlie decided to roll a couple more cigarettes for us. It was almost two o'clock now, so we only had another hour and a half to go before we could go home. Just then, there was a rustle in the grass, and we were silent. We were all like deer in the headlights. Suddenly over the horizon it was Mr. Copeland, he was an ominous looking figure probably because his job was that of truant officer, he was an older man with a full head of grey hair and a stern look on his face. He said sarcastically, "Boys, what you been up to since you've been away, we missed you? Time for you to come with me. Mr. McInnis is looking forward to speaking with you." We were scared. We knew what this all meant when we would be brought in front of the principal. Mr. Copeland put us in his car and drove us to St. Agnes and I was sure I was going to boy's school in Shelburne. Oh God! I began crying for my mom. Wayne was crying a bit as well, Charlie was being stoic about it all. I think he had been down this road a couple of times before and knew what was about to unfold.

We were deposited to Mr. McInnis' office, he took us into his office and lined us up, Then, he walked up and down in front of us, all the time clapping the thick black rubber strap on the palm of his hand, as he was doing this, you could smell the rubber as he stuck the strap on his hand over and over again , all the while pacing back and forth in front of us, looking menacingly at us before finally saying: "So, boys, what do you think I should do?" I was like a newborn baby, bawling and crying as was Wayne, Charlie, still no so much. Mr. McInnis began to call our parents first he called Charlie's mom. *"Hello, just to let you know we found Charlie. Yes, yes, he was playing hooky. I agree, five straps to each hand. Thank you"* Then, he called Wayne's mom, and the conversation was similar. My mother was the last to be called, I was hoping she would take my side plead my case and I'd get a lighter sentence. *"Hello Mrs. Nearing, we found Derrick. Yes, he was playing hooky with the two others. Yes, yes. Well, I am giving the others five straps on each hand."* Suddenly, he held the phone away from his ear, and we could all hear my mom.

"Give the little bastard ten on each hand, then send him home and we give him a little more." He looked at me with a smirk, then the other guys began giggling while looking over at me, I was in it deep and no one to bail me out. We all heard my mother screaming on the phone, and so with tears running down my face, I knew my goose was cooked, and it was going to be the strap.

First, it was Charlie. Mr. McInnis rolled up his sleeves and took Charlie's hand and flattened it out. Then, he wound up, and as he was coming down with the strap, Charlie pulled his hand away and the strap Mr. McInnis right in the leg. Charlie laughed, but this only got the principal more riled up, and he gave him some good hard wacks, but Charlie didn't even budge. Next, it was Wayne, and he took it pretty good, but a few tears fell. Then it was my turn. Heck, I didn't even need to get one strap and I was crying, though I'm not sure if it was for Mr. McInnis and him strapping me, or the thought of facing my mom and dad when I got home. Once the strapping was done, I could feel my hands throbbing in-sync with my heartbeat. Boy, did they hurt and felt some hot from the strapping. I was sure that this would be my first and last attempt and playing hooky.

Mr. McInnis gave us a good talking to and made us promise not to do this again. As I wiped away the tears, I asked about Shelburne. He smiled, and said, "Not this time, Derrick. But don't try this again or who knows?" I still had the long walk home from St. Agnes, down to Heelan Street, and that walk up the hill from the bottom of Heelan St. I was walking so slowly, with my head down, thinking about what I was going to say to mom and dad. I knew that the punishment I received at the school wouldn't be the end of it by no means. Eventually, I would have to make my way home and face the music with mom and dad, I understood what I had done was wrong, that I had embarrassed my parents with my actions and would never do this again.

FIRST COMMUNION

G ROWING UP IN NEW WATERFORD MEANT YOU EITHER WENT to one of the Catholic or public schools, and with our family being Catholic, plus living close to No. 12 Colliery, we were sent to St. Agnes for our elementary schooling. The high school part of schooling changed when they opened BEC in 1973 and the province went to public education. However, even then, the elementary schools stayed loosely divided by religious lines, for another twenty years or so. When I went to St. Agnes, there were two big events during my time there, which were our First Communion and a couple of years later Confirmation. In grade three, the time had come and we were all ready to prepare for and attend our First Communion. I remember our teachers doing the preparations and drilling us with the rote learning of our prayers, and later we would have visits from Father Morley, the parish priest, on the proper way to do confession and how to receive Communion. He also would drill the class with questions, such as "Who was God? Where does God live? Where is God?" There were a couple of months of this, prior to the actual First Communion ceremony.

With our school being next to St. Agnes Church, we were expected to try and attend the early morning Mass before school every day leading up to the First Communion ceremony. Our teacher, Mrs. Aucoin, went every morning, and kept an informal attendance of who was there, and told us if we attended every Mass every day until First Communion that she would give each one of us kids who hadn't missed a Mass, a silver dollar! Unfortunately, I missed one Mass towards the end when I was sick, but that was the deal back then. You had to have perfect attendance for the month prior to First Communion, or you didn't get the silver dollar.

Looking back, I think the main reason I went to Mass every morning was that there was a little girl, Marie, and I guess it was my first inkling that there was something other than boys, wrestling, and the playground. I always tried to sit close to her during morning mass. It was nice just to sit still there in the pews, in the quiet of church with her and all my classmates in deep thought.

Mom had gotten me a little blazer, dress pants, and a perfect boy's haircut from Dave Willkie's Barbershop for First Communion. As the day finally arrived, we had all completed our pre-Communion studies and practices, and it was now time. I remember going to church for the special mass. We all sat up towards the front of the church in the first few pews, the boys' and girls' seating staggered boy, girl, boy, etc. It looked as if we were all involved in group wedding ceremony, the boys with their slacks, blazers, collared shirts, bow ties, and fresh haircuts, and the girls were all beautiful in their white, lacey dresses, veils, and little white gloves.

Bishop Power was conducting the Mass. He seemed larger than life, with the big, gold, ornate robe making him look like he was seven feet tall, especially with his miter, and Father Morley equally dressed in robes, assisting. I can still remember the butterflies in my belly and not wanting to make a mistake in front of Father Morley or the Bishop. Back then, he was the closest thing to God, and you didn't want to make a mistake in front of him. God knows you would probably go straight to hell! The time in the Mass came to go up and get our First Communion, we lined up in two rows, side by side, and I kept thinking, "Don't forget to bow your head and say Amen!"

The altar boys were on either side of the Bishop and Father Morley, and they had what were called the "paten" (Communion plate) on the end of a long wooden pole that they would put under your chin as the wafer was placed on your tongue. This was probably the most stressful part of the whole ceremony, because we were told that if the Communion fell, it would hopefully be onto these plates. The reason you would want it to land on the Communion plate was that we were told if it touched the ground, it would be a big ordeal, the priest had to say prayers, do some sort of ceremony to bless the wafer, then they would have to burn the wafer and all this sort of disposal ceremony. Looking back now, I think it was just to scare us, and I must say they were very successful in doing this!

Once we got our Communion and the Mass had ended, then it was the pictures on the altar, and then individual photos with the bishop, then with Father Morley, then with our parents, then with the bishop, Father Morley, *and* our parents, and then finally the group picture. Holy cow, I think this is where the paparazzi was invented. Although mom and dad didn't have a camera, there were lots of others taking pictures on that day, however, it is strange that with all the pictures taken by friends and family during that time, I only have the one picture of me in my little blazer, which our neighbour was kind enough to take on that day and give to me later in life.

Afterwards, we would go back home, and there would be a little lunch where our relatives would show up and we would get First Communion cards given to us. Some got a little bible, rosary beads, or some memento from the occasion. I remember (and still have) the Communion cards. They are innocent paintings of hands praying, or a little boy or girl dressed in their Sunday best, and inside would be a message of congratulations from a relative or neighbour and a nice, new, green dollar bill.

ST. AGNES
BINGO HALL

ROWING UP ON HEELAN STREET, JUST DOWN FROM WHAT
was called Eaton's corner and was later purchased by St.
Agnes Church to become known as the Parish Hall. This
building, along with the smaller one across the street (now Burkes),
both these buildings belonged to St. Agnes Church. My earliest
memories of these buildings were for two main things, weddings and
bingo! There wasn't a Friday night throughout the year where the streets
around out neighbourhood wouldn't be jammed with cars and people,
coming from all over town and neighboring communities around New
Waterford for their weekly bingo fix. There were also wedding receptions every weekend in the hall. I liked these, because most times the
next day, if you walked around the parking lot early in the morning,
you would find a couple of quarters or dimes or occasionally a dollar
bill. But mostly, I liked the bingo, because it gave me an inside view of
the adult world. When I turned nine years old, I remember some of the
kids in the neighborhood telling me that if I wanted to join them, there
was a way to make a little money, running back and forth to Buddy
Graham's Corner Store for pop, chips, and cigarettes for the men and
women playing bingo.

I couldn't wait to begin and was anxious waiting for Friday to come.
Finally, Friday night arrived, and I was ready to begin my career as a
store runner at the bingo hall. The older kids told me to take the second
floor and to stick to the side, which had the covered stairs going to the
outside of the building next to Gillis' driveway. I watched the other
boys, and how they darted in and out of the aisles, and how they seemed

to know just where to go. I could see that with the other guys being so familiar with the women sitting at the bingo tables, these were the regular customers each of them ran to the store for each week.

When I first went onto the second story floor, it looked gigantic! The bingo hall was three stories high, with the main floor, second floor, and smaller third floor. It was packed to the rafters on most every bingo nights, with people wall to wall. The first thing I remember was the smell of stale beer from the wedding receptions which took place during the week, mixed in with the sweet smell of sugar from the fountain pop. There was a large cloud of cigarette smoke which came billowing out of the bingo hall from every opening, it seemed most everyone smoked during the Bingo games. The lights were bright in the main hall, where men and women sat at the six-foot tables with what seemed and unmanageable amount of bingo cards in front of them. The game hadn't begun, and you could hear a low buzz throughout the building. It sounded like bees in a beehive, with everyone talking at once, drinking their pop, and eating their chips and candy bars, with an occasional puff of a cigarette in between bites.

I think for the few in the crowd, it was about winning the weekly jackpot, which would slowly build each week when not won, but for most it was about the social aspect I believe. They paid between five and seven dollars, and it was a chance to get out for the night, to gossip, to meet old friends in a weekly routine and have time away from their husbands and kids, to take off the weight of the week they'd had.

When I began my career as a store runner, it was on the second floor, where I began and would stay for the duration of my store runner career. On my initial night, the first people I saw were two of my grandaunts, and they were in the area I would be going to the store for. Right away, I saw Beattie, Francie, Mary Jane, Jeanette, and some other ladies I was familiar with, as they sat at the table talking and chatting. When they spotted me, Francie waved her hand, motioning for me to come over to them. I was amazed when I got to the tables; they must have had sixteen to twenty cards each in front of them, and they all had their own little lucky charms out. For some, above the top of their cards, would be lucky a rabbit's foot or a rosary. There were some lucky pennies, or the wearing of a lucky sweater. You could tell a few of the ladies would be saying a novena, and if you could read lips, you would know that the "Our Father" prayer was being recited silently, especially as more numbers got called and their cards were almost full.

Once the game begun the numbers came over the speaker system. B–7, then a ten second pause, N–43, and again, another pause. And this would go on until there was a call of BINGO! Usually men from the KOC were on each floor acting as floor supervisors for when a bingo was called, and next to them was a button that sounded a buzzer down to the number caller to indicate there may be a winner.

Throughout the bingo hall during the game, you would hear the continual buzz of the ladies talking in between numbers, with a few laughs, but all in a seamless coordinated dance. I never knew how they did this, watch sixteen-twenty cards, eat, smoke, and drink their pop, cover their numbers, and do all this in such a coordinated manner. The talk was kept low, so they could hear the numbers over the conversation.

As the floor walker would call the number downstairs to the caller, they would be repeated, and through all of this, there would be the ongoing conversations, but always with half an ear to hear the bingo being confirmed, as they swept their cards away for the next game. However, occasionally, someone would call bingo prematurely. You would hear from the caller, "*O-sixty-seven?? No, there is no O-sixty-seven. This number was not called.*" Then, it would be a look from the crowd that could kill a horse. Many had already cleared off their cards and were now out of that game as the number caller continued, unless they could mark them again by looking at another's cards. The person who had made the wrong call might as well had leprosy and leave right then, there would be a silent shame the rest of the night and often into the next evening.

One night, there were so many people smoking that one the neighbours, close to the Bingo Hall, called the fire department as they thought the building was on fire, with one of them actually going over and pulling the alarm to empty everyone out the building. I looked around, and there was an old lady they were trying to convince to come out. She was saying, "*Jesus Christ, call the damn numbers, I only need one more number for a full card. Just finish the game.*" Finally, a couple of the men from the KOC picked her up and took her out, her little legs kicking all the way down the stairs to everyone's laugh's.

Throughout the evening we darted in and out of the side entrance like Olympic sprinters, attentive to customers looks, a raised eyebrow or wave of a finger and off we would go. Then. the orders for the store: "*get me a Pepsi, bag of chips, and a pack of cigarettes*", said one. And then next would give her order, and then the next. They would each give us the money, and we ran up to Buddy Graham's with our list in mind, and get the two or three orders we had. Then, we'd pay for each one separately and head off back to the bingo hall to deliver the goods. Once we got back, we would count out the exact change to the ladies, and they would give us a nickel or a dime. We would ask them for their bottle when they were finished and if they said no problem we would pick it up when empty. Each bottle was worth three cents each at the time, so this was money we would bank in our minds, to be collected at the end of the night when we brought the bottles back to the store.

As the night went on, there were fewer orders, and we would start getting a wave to come and take away the pop bottles. As we were picking up the pop bottles, we made little piles, each of us had our collections of bottles, and no one ever stepped on another's turf or took bottles that weren't theirs, even if the bingo patrons waved the wrong runner over. These days are sadly no more, but thinking back I am humbled with these experiences and the lessons taught to me during the time I was a store runner for the bingo hall.

THANKFUL FOR THANKSGIVING

I REMEMBER AS A CHILD GETTING UP EARLY ON THANKSGIVING MORN-
ings. There was the smell of turkey and ham in the air, wafting up
through the grates in our bedroom floor upstairs. Mom was busy in
the kitchen, preparing the turkey and ham, peeling the potatoes, carrots,
and turnips, and soaking them in cold water.

The day prior, mom had made an apple pie and put out into the back
porch to cool overnight. In those days, the back porch was used during
the fall, winter, and spring as an overflow refrigerator. Everything was
clean and tidy in the house as Mom had cleaned a day earlier. Dad must
have been up early and taken out the ashes and had the fire stoked up
so high, it felt like summer's heat had returned. My brother Kim and I
were still snuggled in our beds, and the bedroom window opened just a
little, with the cool fresh air blowing in through the bedroom, it seemed
just the right temperature.

More than anything else, I still remember that aroma of the turkey
cooking all through the house. Even now as a parent with my own
family, I rise early to prepare the potato stuffing mixed with poultry sea-
soning, this reawakens my memories from childhood in Cape Breton,
and then the five hours or so of it cooking in the oven, occasionally
taking it out to baste and check it, these are the smells that awaken
childhood memories. Once the turkey and fixings were ready, it was the
presentation that was important, and mom had the table always looking
so prim and proper, with the cranberries and the main attraction, the
turkey. With this, we were ready to eat. We just needed poor Mom to
take some time and sit with us. I've noticed growing older how often

moms never get to eat a proper meal. They are always busily preparing, cooking, tasting, baking, getting the table ready, then serving the meal. By the time mom did all this, she had lost her appetite from picking and tasting all day.

30 years later at my home in Pembroke, I still have Mom's old cookbook. It is an old, green, bristle-board covering and typed out, copied on a mimeograph machine. A couple hundred of these books would be made and sold by the St. Agnes CWL, to raise money for new choir books or something needed for the church. My wife, Maureen, laughs at me every time I cook or bake and she sees me pull out this old ripped, worn out recipe book, about 40 years old or more now. To myself, it is a reminder of my mom, this old book is my connection to my past, with my mom and dad, my brothers and sisters, my friends, and my neighbours. To be honest, it's mostly everything that reminds me of home.

It's an especially good memory tool when it's used to cook, and my memory is once again awoken with gentle reminders of mom's cooking. Such as the time I came home from being outside playing all day to the aroma of a freshly baked roast with gravy, potatoes, and peas. Just before supper, dad would walk through the front door from work and us children running up to him and giving a hug and kissing his cheek. The feel of his short prickly whiskers tickling my face, and then as I hugged him, burying my face into his thick felt jacket, the smell of the fresh winters air mixed with the smells from coal mine and bar soap he used to shower with coming out of the mine, all these scents were still hanging on in his jacket from the long walk home after his shift.

When my younger brother Kevin comes to visit us now, he always calls a couple of days ahead and asks me to cook the same food mom used to cook. I get to work by first taking out my Cape Breton Cookbook and looking at what mom made that he liked best. Then I begin by baking some cookies, a lemon loaf, and a banana loaf. Later in the day, I prepare some cabbage rolls and a lasagna. On the day of his arrival, I stuff the turkey and everything that makes eating a turkey special—the beets, potato stuffing, carrots, mashed potatoes, and to top it all off, turnip with a dab of butter! I can always tell whether I have done well after the meal, with Kevin's smile of approval and loosening of the belt and a little nap.

Like mom, I always cook a 12-pound turkey, because Thanksgiving isn't just the Sunday. I make more than we need for one meal, so then it carries on into the next day, with hot turkey sandwiches and gravy, with some of the leftover vegetables. But even after it's seemingly all gone, it's not! There's the turkey bones and some of the skin and meat, which will be boiled into a stock for a delicious turkey soup. Amazing, these things I lovingly learned from my mom.

I went home a week prior to mom's passing, and we had some alone time, just her and me that week, and she kept on asking me if she had been a good mother to all of us, if she'd done a good job. She was afraid, and angry, because what happened to her with the cancer and how it had come so fast. I told her how much I loved her, and how important she'd been in keeping the family going all these years, from trying to raise all us kids in those early years, then in dealing with dad's early death, leaving her with us five kids, the two younger ones being only six and eight years old at the time of dad's passing. We talked about her life of trying to live on a meager miner's pension and raise children, I reminded her that she did it, she made the best of it and did a great job as a mom, I then told her she should be proud of all she had accomplished raising us children and running a house. Mom needed to hear this before she died, she needed to know that we were going to be ok and she got us to where we needed to be.

On Thanksgiving, I usually think of my mother and father, I am forever thankful for all the love and kindness they had put into myself and my brothers and sisters, so we could become who we are today. For sure their life it wasn't all smooth, but the basics of kindness and love were put in place for us and have served us well as we have made our way through life, now carrying on these lessons they had given us while raising our own families.

ST. AGNES JANITOR

A FEW WEEKS AGO, I WAS LOOKING AT SOME PICTURES FROM my days at St. Agnes Elementary school. I began to think about our janitor there, Ray MacLean. Every morning on my arrival, he would be down in the little stationary room he worked out of, by the gym, always pleasant and smiling as he greeted us. The two most important people in a school, as every parent knows, are the school secretary and the janitor. I remember looking at Ray and thinking to myself how amazing he was, a quiet professional. Most people would never give the school janitor a second look, and although I didn't fully understand his significance to my education at the time, I somehow knew that he was an important piece of the puzzle in my early education.

I recently looked up the meaning of the word "janitor," and it comes from the Latin word "ianitor," or "Janus," and it means "doorkeeper." The god of doorways in ancient Rome was called Ianus, "Janus," and he had two faces, one looked to the past and the other to the future. When you think of it, the job of school janitor comes with all the keys to the school, some hefty responsibilities in making sure the school is open and ready for the kids in the morning, the locking at the end of the day, and being there at all hours for First Communions, Confirmations, school concerts, dances, and occasional community use. So, for Ray the title of "janitor" was a fitting one.

Ray oversaw painting the classroom during the summer, making sure the heat plant was working, fixing doors and locks, windows, lockers, pencil sharpeners, and so much more. But I remember one thing that always impressed me during my time at old St. Agnes, the hardwood floor in the gym. Every couple of years, Ray would strip, sand, and varnish the floor, and I remember going up and sitting outside the big double doors by the floor at the entrance, and watching how he did this with such dedication and attention to detail. I remember his sons would be there helping him, words were used economically, it was work with a purpose. He and the boys were amazing in how they painted the lines, measuring out all the different court markings for basketball, volleyball, and badminton then once these lines dried, the final coat of high gloss varnish, it was beautiful.

Ray, as most janitors I imagine, through observing his work had given me and others so many teachable moments. There were those who said, He is just a janitor," or maybe never even noticed him, failed to realize that he was the beginning and end for our school life. As soon as we left at the end of the day, he would sweep every room, wash and wax the floors, empty out all the trash buckets, and clean the bathrooms. On returning in the morning, all we would see was a sparkling clean school, and the smell of pencil lead, crayons, and a little dust bane. But we were kids and knew no better, we thought that somehow it was always like this. However, It was his hard work and dedication to the school that made it so.

The first lesson he taught me was that everyone is valuable and contributes, so don't take people for granted. When I entered the building going to school, Ray would always there with a kind smile, a wave, and a hello. In this simple act, he was teaching us all about respect and politeness. His being kind to us kids, paving the way for the rest of our day at the school. Later, when I joined the army and posted to Petawawa, I would notice that some of the guys would make fun of and belittle the janitor at our unit because of her station in life. However, every morning when I would arrive at work, I always had a coffee for her and a smile as she began her day. Ray taught me that everyone deserves to be respected, and that we are all part of the same team no matter how much or how little we contribute.

Ray, and all the hard workers like him, had come into my life over the years, taught me not to take people for granted, that they have an impact on us which we may never fully know or understand, until someone opens our eyes to it. Think back to all those silent professionals you never took the time to notice, those who enabled you to succeed at work, take a moment to acknowledge them and don't overlook them.

With Ray's quiet demeanor, he taught me to stay hungry and stay humble. Up until my very last day in the military, I worked. When I completed my last fitness test, I could have chosen not to attempted it, as it no longer mattered for my employment of being in the military, as I was retiring. But on the day of the physical fitness test, I completed it with the rest of the troops and passed. Ray's work ethic and the things he accomplished around the school, such as the yearly painting of the gym floor and having the school always so perfectly clean, taught me to not look back on past accomplishments, but to be pleased with what you've achieved and use these little successes to work harder and improve for next time. I saw this in him, emulated it, and left my last day at work with my head held high, as Ray's example taught me.

During my career I always worked hard, because Rays example taught me that it is our work that defines who we are, and any rewards deserved will follow. Ray's example of hard work taught me that no job is above or below, anyone. The lesson is in the fact that no matter your lot in life, you should excel at whatever you do, and no job is beneath us. When I was deployed to Somalia back in 1993, when we used the washroom, it would be in a 45-gallon drum, cut in half due to the austere conditions on that tour. At the end of each day, one of us would be sent add gas and diesel to the drum to burn the waste off, stirring it as it burned. This was our only way of doing sanitation. When I did this task, I did so with a sense of duty, because it was for the good of all of us. It was to preserve our health and I was not above taking my turn at this task. Throughout my career, there were many jobs such as this, but never was there one beneath my dignity. I saw this displayed in Ray's work ethic, day in and day out and the example he set for us.

He taught me to be patient and watch for my opportunities, to be the person who everyone wants on their team, to make myself invaluable not by what you say, rather by what you do. I remember being called back to my unit in 1994 to go to Rwanda on only a day's notice. Was I the best or smartest soldier, possibly not? But one thing my supervisors knew was that I was the hardest working, and they knew that nothing would stop me, and the job would get done. This drive for me to work, had been witnessed day in and day out for the first seven years of my schooling at St. Agnes, so I understood the need for hard work.

As I had some success throughout my life, and career in the military, people would occasionally ask me who I modelled myself after. With this question, I usually pause and think of all the hard-working men and women I witnessed throughout my life growing up in Cape Breton. Every single day of my early life, from the time I can remember, until I left home for good, it was those coal miners, war widows, grocery baggers, janitors, and so many more. They are still there today, around all of us, if we but take the time to stop, look and listen to the lessons they offer. Yes, Ray MacLean was a janitor, but he was no less a teacher, mentor, and friend to all of us who walked through the halls and class-rooms of St. Agnes Elementary School and every school then and now, still has these heroes within its walls.

THE LITTLE
BLUE BIKE

HAD A SCOOTER FOR MOST OF MY CHILDHOOD UP UNTIL GRADE three. Then, at the end of that year, things changed. I was in Ms. Sandra McNeil's class that year and went to school on that last day of June, and at the end of the afternoon when the last buzzer of the school year rang, it sounded off the beginning of summer. I wished Ms. McNeil a good summer, grabbed my report card, and took off running for home to show mom and dad. Along the way home, I stopped in a few homes to show my report card. I was so proud that I had passed. I remember Mrs. Timmons congratulating me and giving me a quarter, then Mrs. Stanford telling me how smart I was and another quarter. I did this a few more times and got a few more quarters before heading home.

I burst into the front doors and screamed, "MOMMY, DADDY, I PASSED!"

Dad was in bed, as he had just gotten home from day shift at the mine, and mom was in the kitchen with the old clothes washer. Mom stopped what she was doing for a minute and looked at me and said, "Wait a minute. I have to get dad." Then mom and dad appeared and said to me, "Come on outside, Derrick. We have a little surprise for you."

I waited on the veranda while dad went out to the back yard, only to return with a shiny, blue, banana-seat bicycle. It was a beautiful bike. Mom and dad were saying something in the background, but I couldn't hear them. I was too busy falling in love with the bike. It was blue, with while forks, and they had attached multi-coloured streamers onto the handgrips. There was the red reflector underneath the seat, and one in the spokes on the front wheel. Wow, this was it, I thought. I was finally rid of the scooter and onto my very first bicycle.

This day, I remember vividly, because it was my first day with something that would liberate me and allow me to explore the neighbourhood and the town, to ride back and forth to school in the fall. So many possibilities were there for me, I couldn't wait. I had never really ridden a bike before, and there were no training wheels on this one, but it was like I was made to ride this bike.

As soon as my right foot touched the pedal, I put pressure on the pedal, and it went down, then the left, then right, slowly moving forward in those tentative first few moments. I fell and scraped my elbows and knees and began to sob a little, but I was determined not to let this get in my way and picked myself up, wiped away the tears and hopped back on and tried again and then again until I could smoothly push the pedals and move forward. By the end of day, I was doing slides in the dirt and popping wheelies. It was great, exhilarating to finally be set free.

Now that I had my bike, I could ride up to see my mom's aunts, Francie and Beattie, or my Aunt Lucille on Baker Avenue. It was great, because what used to take twenty minutes to walk, I could now do in two minutes, at least it felt that way. I remember myself and all the other boys being annoying, zipping in and out of people up by the band shell next to the Miners Monument as a band was playing. Looking back, I am certain we were irritating, but tolerated. As the summer went on, I got more adventurous, and with the guys on Second Street, we would build a little ramp and try to be like Evel Knievel, jumping over one, two, then three of our friends, before someone would end up getting squished, and then it would be over. We would also learn how to ride "double," that is, to have another kid sitting on your crossbar as you rode.

One day, mom asked me to run up to Buddy Graham's Store for her, I hopped on my bike and went up and got the bread, milk, and a pack of Zig Zag tobacco for her. On the way back down Plummer avenue, the chain fell off the front sprocket connected to the pedals and I couldn't stop! The bike went faster, faster, faster down the hill, and by then, I was riding into the intersection of Plummer Ave and Heelan Street, when suddenly there was a loud screeching of brakes being locked, followed by a "CRASH!", which was me being hit.

A car coming up the street had hit me, sending me flying over the handlebars, going face first, banging my head off the pavement. My head hurt and my nose was bleeding and shoulder sore, but right away, I jumped up. The guy driving the car and his girlfriend hopped out right away, trying to get me lay down and wait for an ambulance, but I wouldn't have anything to do with this. I ran over to my bike, unconcerned with myself at the time, it was as if my bike was a living, breathing person. Looking down at it laying there all twisted, I began to cry when I saw how badly it was damaged.

I picked it up and walked it home, with the frame now twisted and the back wheel skipping along as it cold no longer turn. As soon as I saw my mom, the crying got worse and I couldn't stop crying. Mom and dad got me this bike for grading day, and now it was all ruined. As I was feeling so bad, and tears streaming down my face because of what I had done, mom told me it was ok and asked me where I hurt. Just her love and squeezing me comforted me and took away some of the pain. Then she called Claire Timmons down the street and they took me to the hospital. I was seen there in the New Waterford Consolidated Hospital by Dr. Nathanson, who took x-rays, then examined me, and finally told mom I had a concussion, but the egg on my forehead would eventually go away and there was no need to worry.

A day or two later, the young fellow and his girlfriend dropped by the house. I remember his name was Joe, and he offered to buy me a new bike. Mom told him that would be nice, but even a second had bike would be good enough because, after all, she had bought my first one second hand. So that afternoon, Joe and his girlfriend showed up and presented me with a "new" second hand bike. Although a different model from the blue one mom and dad had given me, it was still a beauty of a bike, all red with a white banana seat and white wall tires, brand new tires to be exact with lots of rubber on them for squealing when I applied the brakes. And with that, I was off to find new adventures once again. Along with being given the "new" bike that day, also came second chances, the chance to have not been seriously injured and live a long and fulfilling life, the chance to be given another bike so I could continue with exploring my little town of New Waterford, and finally the chance to continue doing what kids should do and have fun exploring and finding new adventure.

BAKING BREAD
WITH NANNY

REMEMBER THOSE TIMES WHEN MOM AND DAD TAKE US CHILDREN every Saturday over to Dominion. We would go for a visit with Uncle Freddie and Nanny. They were my mother's aunt and uncle. They who helped raise mom after her mother died, around 1953. With my grandmother's death before I was born, my mother and her brother, Wayne, were raised by the family. Looking back to these times, I never really had a grandmother on either side of my parents' families. But Nanny was my grandmother's older sister, and I guess by default she was the closest to a grandmother I would ever know. Nanny, and her brother Freddie, lived on Church Street, Dominion in a small and humble home. Her name was Evelyn, and I believe she was the oldest of Mom's aunts, all those aunts who helped to raise her and her brother.

I treasured visiting them, and it would last for most of the day, what with the drive over and then being set lose to run around Dominion to visit all my uncles, aunts, and cousins. While we were doing this, mom and dad would spend time with Nanny and Freddie, catching up over a cup of tea. Kim, Andrea, and I would visit everyone and feel the warm embrace of our cousins. It was the comfort of the clan, to be with those who all came from the same blood. They were all genuine people, nothing false about them.

I always loved going to their old house. It was a small, two-story house, with blue shingles and a white trim. The house was extremely small by todays standards, with only a kitchen and front room on the first floor and the pantry under the staircase. Upstairs were two modest bedrooms with a diminutive bathroom and even smaller third bedroom, used mostly for storage.

Returning from visiting our aunts, uncles, and cousins, we would enter the house from the back porch, and smells from the kitchen wafted into our face, as the aroma of the yeast coming from a large, covered, rubber bowl greeted us. When we would enter, she would always have that beautiful smile, greeting us. Nanny always wore a dress and apron and her long hair would be pulled back neatly with an elastic, as she sat in her usual spot over at the end of the kitchen table, by the small single tub sink, which only had a cold-water tap, as hot water had to be boiled. Her hands were big and strong, spread out with rough callouses along the palms from the years of hard work, yet so gentle when she would hold your face in those hands and kiss you on the cheek on arriving to visit. You could tell her hands had seen years of hard work, to look at her hands one could tell of her history and the difficult life they came through, from the depression, World War II, Korea and the life of living in a coal mining town.

My brother Kim would still be over visiting with our cousin Brian, while Andrea would be in the front room, playing with her dolls. As the adults talked, I watched across from the pantry, the beehive of activity going on within the kitchen with Uncle Freddie's getting the stove stoked up and preparing the oven, Nanny taking that big bowl of dough and kneading it, rolling, and rolling it again until it was smooth, then and pulling out a slab and cutting it away from the bowl and placing it into a greased bread pan. She would repeat this procedure many times, until she had all the pans ready for the oven. Then, with a piece of wax paper, scoop up some butter and rub it along the top of the bread, prior to baking. I think most of my favorite memories of growing up in Cape Breton were associated with food. I believe this is so because food was always connected with love, family, and sharing. Nanny's bread was the glue that held my own mother's memories together with Nanny and her time growing up in Dominion. As the bread was baking, I could feel my mouth water. Nanny's homemade bread was the high point of our visit on those days.

Uncle Freddie and Nanny would always be doing something as we visited. I can still see Uncle Freddie, with his cigarette making machine, making up his weekly supply of cigarettes. While Nanny would take up her spot, sitting by the kitchen stove while the bread baked, rhythmically rocking in her old oak rocking chair as she spoke with mom and dad, all the time watching the wall clock above the kitchen table, knowing exactly when to take out the bread.

When it was ready, it would be slid out and placed over a rack on the kitchen table. All the loaves were topped with a light brown crust. When she would cut the bread, the inside was glowing white and so soft and tender. She would smooth on thick a wad of butter and molasses, then we would sit there, eating this with our eyes closed, as if it were a treat like no other, in fact it really was a treat like no other. Nanny usually made a couple extra loaves when we came over, for us to take home. I think all the kids in the neighbourhood could smell Nanny's bread baking, as within no time, our cousins from the neighbourhood would show up, and Nanny would give them a piece of bread with butter on it, as she had done for us. She and Uncle Freddie were people of modest means, but they always had a piece of bread for a child.

COAL MINERS'
CHECK NUMBER

WENT THROUGH SOME OLD STORAGE BOXES ON A RAINY WET weekend in my basement awhile back and came across a lump of coal from thirty-five years ago. I had picked it up after my fathers passing, up in the field where No. 12 Colliery use to stand. What I also found while looking around these old storage boxes, was a miner's signal lamp, a metal lunchbox, and my fathers old brass check number from the Development Coal Company (Devco), from when he worked at Lingan Coal Mine.

Dad's check number brings me back to some of the best memories of my father, and with us living so close to No. 12 Colliery Coal Mine. This little piece of brass has so much significance attached to it. If you were to hold it in your hand, it would mean very little to the uninitiated. It is an unassuming, octagonal shaped piece of brass with the company name punched on the top and a number that each miner was assigned and identified them. My father's check number was 3699. There was also a hole punched at the top of the brass coin, where it could be hung on the tally board in the lamp house.

Back in the day, the miners used it when going into the coal mine, as they passed through the lamp house on their way to the boxcars into the mine. It was a way of accounting for the lamps that went out, and in this way, also accounted for the miners who were underground. This was important in the event of a cave in or explosion, a simple but effective visual way to see who was missing during an emergency. A quick glance by the underground manager of the tally board could tell a lot, it was used as a tally for the number of coal cars coming up from the deep, and to account for how much each miner had loaded, so they could get paid for the work they did. These little pieces of brass, although rudimentary and simple in design, became a part of the fiber for the colliery.

When a miner finished his shift, he would exchange his lamp to be recharged on the lamp rack and received his check number back, where it would return home with him. When I was a little boy and was getting up and getting ready to go to school in the morning, the first thing I would look to see when I went downstairs in the morning, was dad's metal lunchbox with his check number next to it. There was comfort in this, comfort knowing he was home, because even as children, we were aware of the dangers of what our fathers did, the dangers of going twelve miles under the ocean. There was also the going through of his lunch box. I remember the smell of the coal and the mine that would rise out of the lunch box when I first opened it. It was a sulphur odour mixed with coal dust and stale bread and it made an impression on my scent memory of childhood. Then, I would go through it and see if there were anything left. Usually, Dad left half of a stale sandwich, which I would take it and eat it, pretending I was on break in the coal mine having my lunch. These are the things a six-year-old does.

The other thing that the check number represented was a deal negotiated by the miners with the provincial government, where Cape Breton Coal Miners would have received provincial healthcare (a precursor to Medicare) through a mandatory check-off insurance plan, some thirty years before the passage of the Canada Health Act. The check off provided deductions from the coal miners salaries, and for this they were guaranteed to receive healthcare for themselves and their families, access to a doctoring, pharma care, and hospital stays. Amazing, when one thinks that coal miners were the leaders in this area until the birth of the National Medicare System in 1967.

However, the simple check number means more than just a piece of brass or healthcare, it means commitment and dedication to family and community. In those days, it was the miners who built and paid for anything the community wanted or needed. Whether that be a church, a hospital, or a rink. These men of the deep, making meagre wages, would do what was called "check off." Simply put, the check off was where every miner would sign off, through their check number, that from each pay cheque, a dollar or two would be taken to pay for a project which would benefit the entire community. The last thing I remember being built with this method in New Waterford was the local rink. Each miner wanted their sons and daughters to be able to skate and play hockey.

Amazing to think that miners, making poverty wages, would be the philanthropic drivers to build small towns all over Cape Breton, build an entire island, build essential services, churches, hospitals, schools, and show a spirit of community and of giving that the workers of today would be hard pressed to emulate. It was a different time, a time of doing what was the best for the collective community, and of sacrificing individual desires for the greater good. I am glad that I was born during this time in the sixties and experienced what now in retrospect would be considered a hard and austere upbringing. The truth is that it was a loving and kind way for children to be raised by a community.

The final gesture of this check off, I was to witness, occurred when my father passed away. As happened when any miner died or was severely injured, the miners would take a collection for the three working shifts of the mine, day shift, night shift and back shift. Each miner would be told what date the collection would take place, and they would bring a small donation, and as the shifts cycled through the day come in and out of the coal mine, the money would be collected at the lamp house as they put their check numbers on the tally board. Dad, who had stomach cancer, worked in the mine up until he died, even with him knowing he was dying he still had to work to feed us, as there were not the benefits then that we have today. After dad passed at fifty-nine years old, the miners at Lingan Coal Mine did this type of check off one last time for my dad. The day after the collection, Mel Quinn, who was one of my father's closest friends, came to the house and gave my mother, newly widowed with children to raise, the $2300 collected from the miners an extremely kind and generous gesture of community support.

Although we perhaps never realized it, we had very little growing up in material goods, but an abundance of love and support. It was a time that was much different then now, a time when the community shared what little they had with one another, a time where mothers and fathers were driven to give everything they had so their children could have the life they never could. A time that made us who we are, who we continue to be, no matter where we live today. I will always be grateful for growing up in New Waterford and hold on to these memories that have given me strength as I have travelled so far through this life.